My Body in Pieces

Published in English in Canada and the USA in 2021 by Groundwood Books
First published in French in 2019 by Les Éditions XYZ inc., coll. Quai n°5
Original title: *La grosse laide*

Groundwood Books / House of Anansi Press
groundwoodbooks.com

Groundwood Books respectfully acknowledges that the land on which we operate is the Traditional Territory of many Nations, including the Anishinabeg, the Wendat and the Haudenosaunee. It is also the Treaty Lands of the Mississaugas of the Credit.

We gratefully acknowledge for their financial support of our publishing program the Canada Council for the Arts, the Ontario Arts Council and the Government of Canada.

Canada Council for the Arts | Conseil des Arts du Canada

ONTARIO ARTS COUNCIL
CONSEIL DES ARTS DE L'ONTARIO
an Ontario government agency
un organisme du gouvernement de l'Ontario

With the participation of the Government of Canada
Avec la participation du gouvernement du Canada | Canada

Library and Archives Canada Cataloguing in Publication
Title: My body in pieces / Marie-Noëlle Hébert ; translated by Shelley Tanaka.
Other titles: Grosse laide. English
Names: Hébert, Marie-Noëlle, author, artist. | Tanaka, Shelley, translator.
Description: Translation of: La grosse laide.
Identifiers: Canadiana (print) 20200267388 | Canadiana (ebook) 2020026768X | ISBN 9781773064840 (hardcover) | ISBN 9781773064857 (EPUB) | ISBN 9781773064864 (Kindle)
Subjects: LCSH: Hébert, Marie-Noëlle—Comic books, strips, etc. | LCSH: Hébert, Marie-Noëlle—Juvenile literature. | LCSH: Overweight persons—Comic books, strips, etc. | LCSH: Overweight persons—Juvenile literature. | LCSH: Self-esteem—Comic books, strips, etc. | LCSH: Self-esteem—Juvenile literature. | LCGFT: Autobiographical comics. | LCGFT: Graphic novels.
Classification: LCC PN6733.H43 G7613 2021 | DDC j741.5/971—dc23

The illustrations were done in graphite.

Printed and bound in China

FSC
www.fsc.org
MIX
Paper from responsible sources
FSC® C008047

My Body in Pieces

By Marie-Noëlle Hébert

Translated by Shelley Tanaka

GROUNDWOOD BOOKS
HOUSE OF ANANSI PRESS
TORONTO / BERKELEY

For Maeva

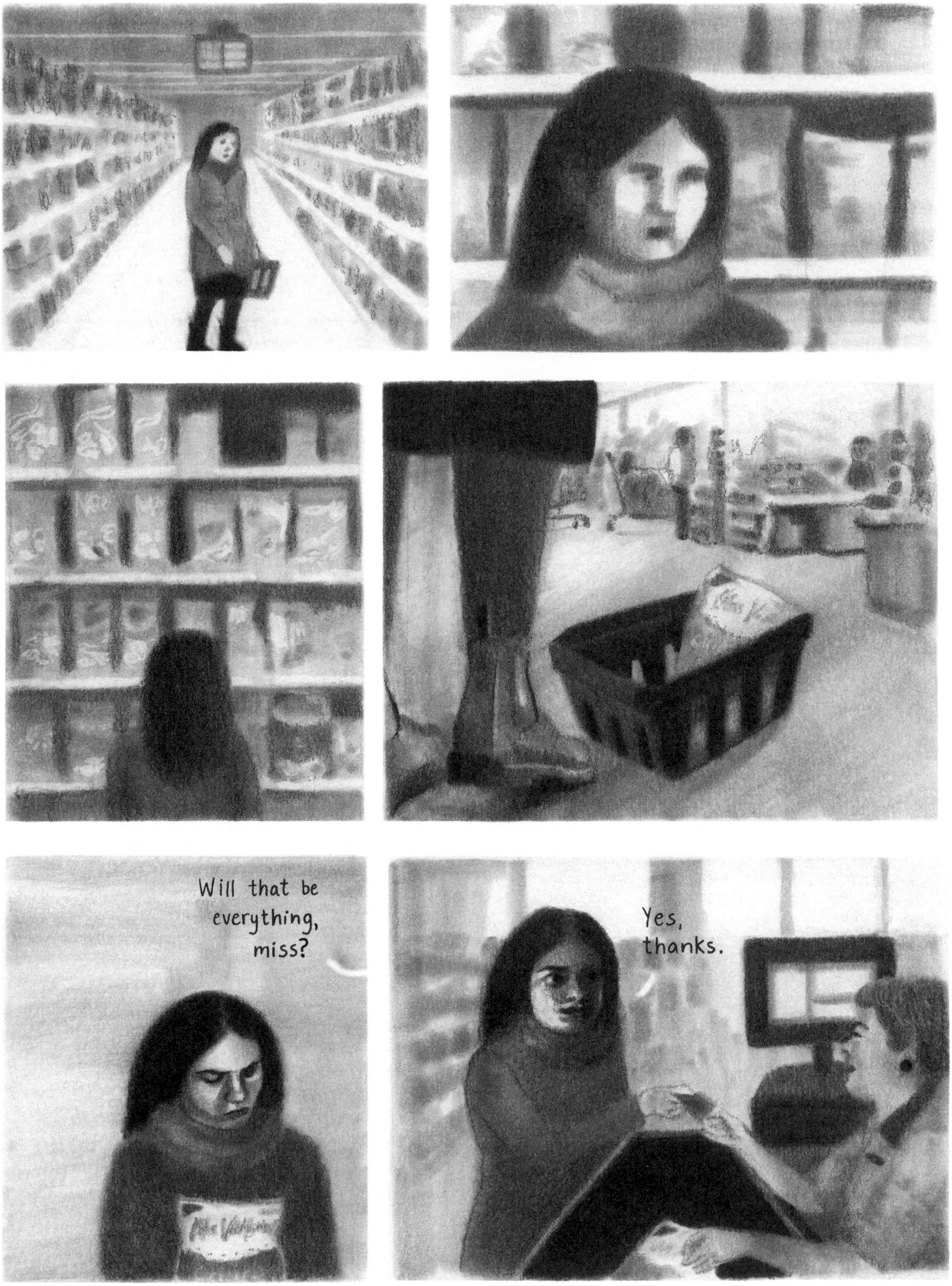
Will that be everything, miss?
Yes, thanks.

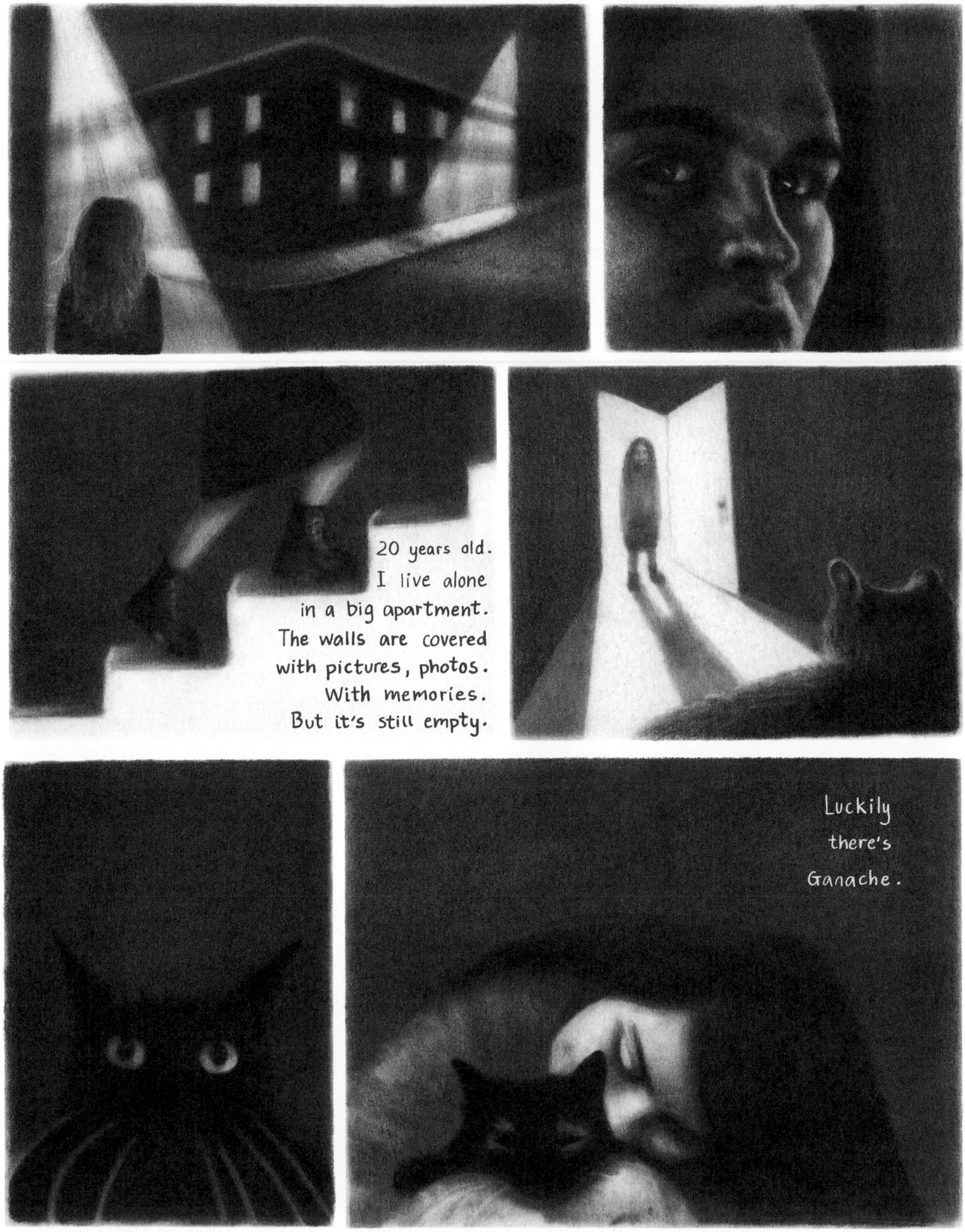
20 years old.
I live alone
in a big apartment.
The walls are covered
with pictures, photos.
With memories.
But it's still empty.
Luckily
there's
Ganache.

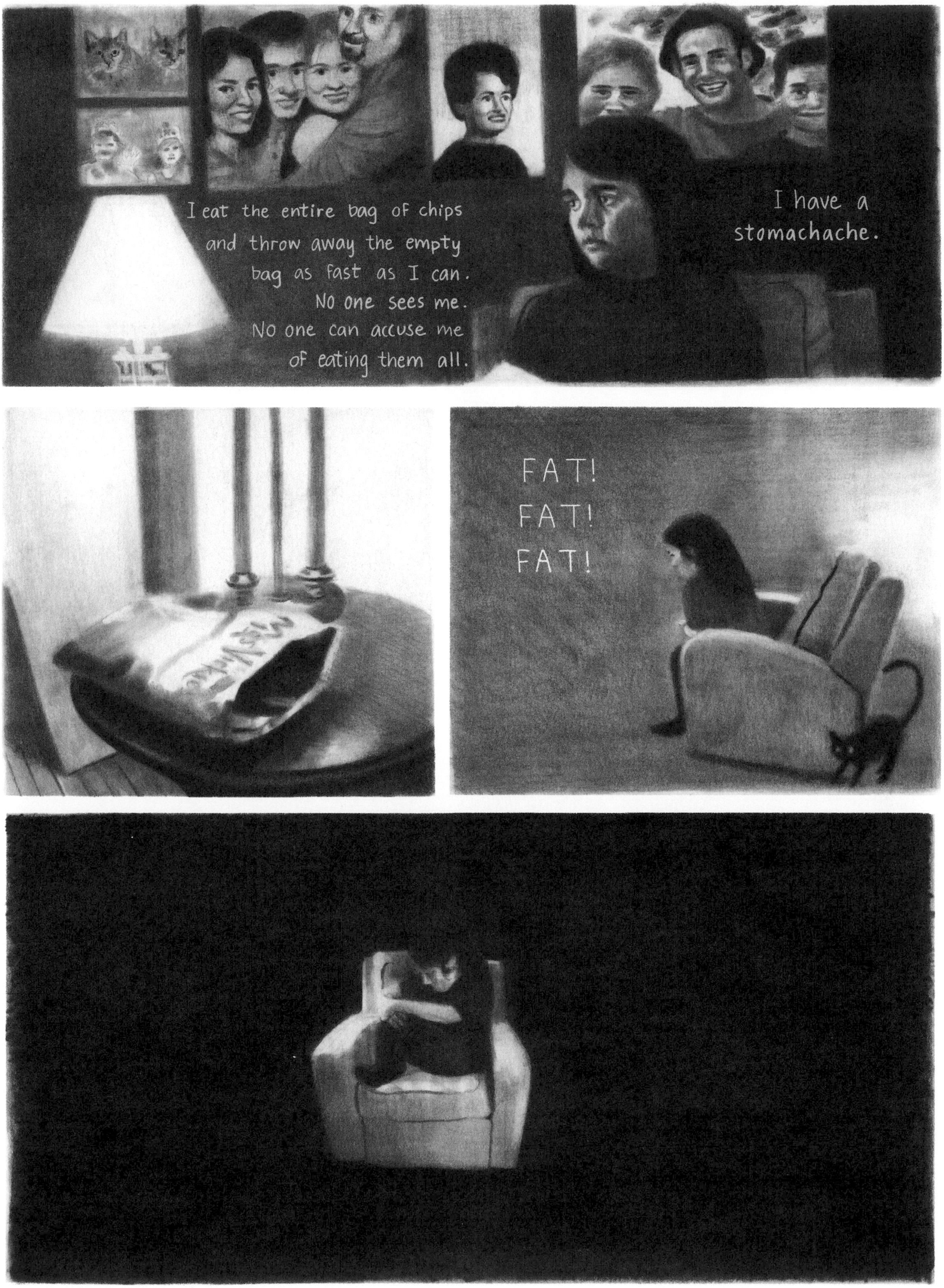
I eat the entire bag of chips and throw away the empty bag as fast as I can. No one sees me. No one can accuse me of eating them all.
I have a stomachache.
FAT! FAT! FAT!

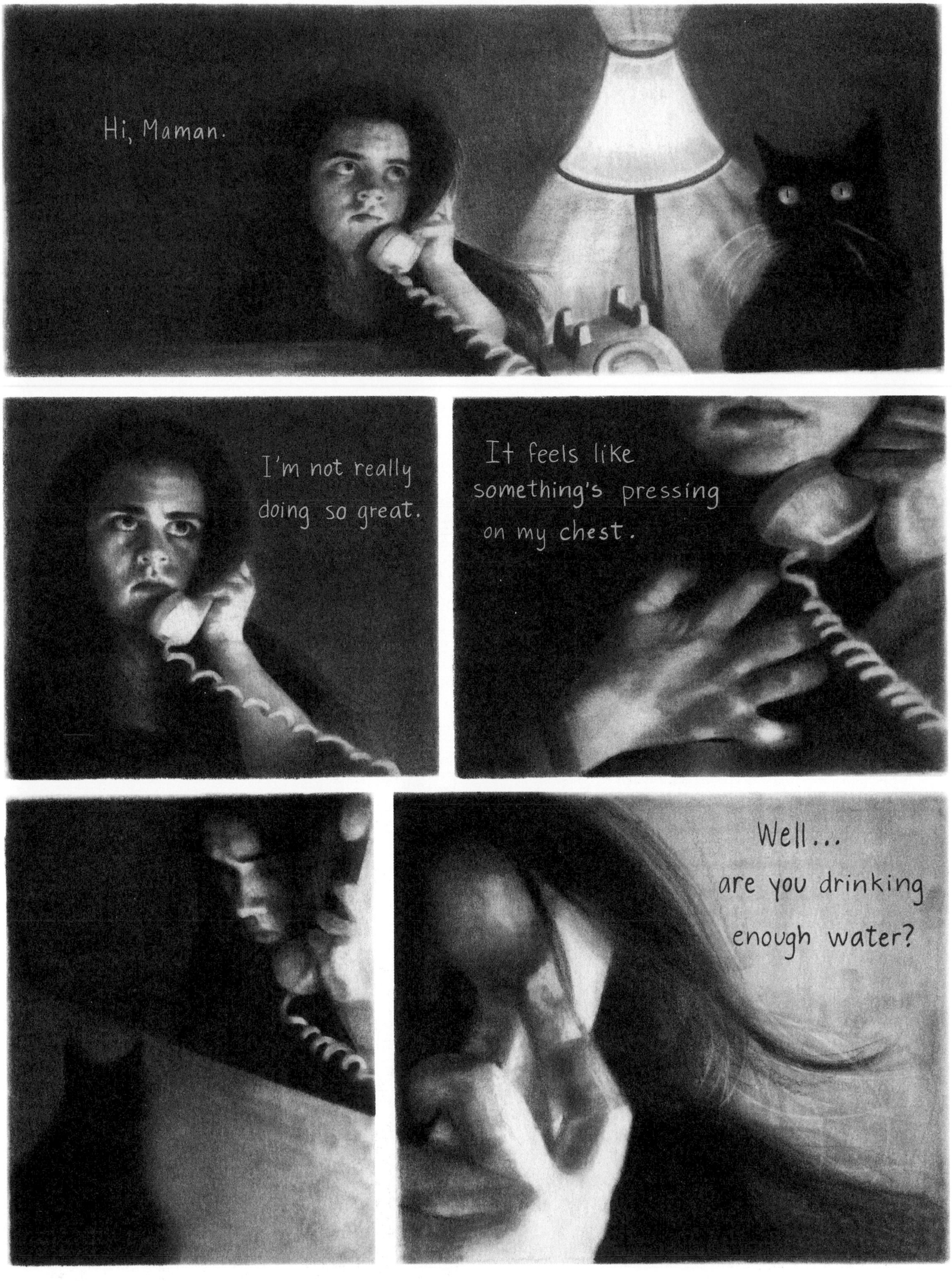
Hi, Maman.
I'm not really doing so great.
It feels like something's pressing on my chest.
Well...
are you drinking enough water?

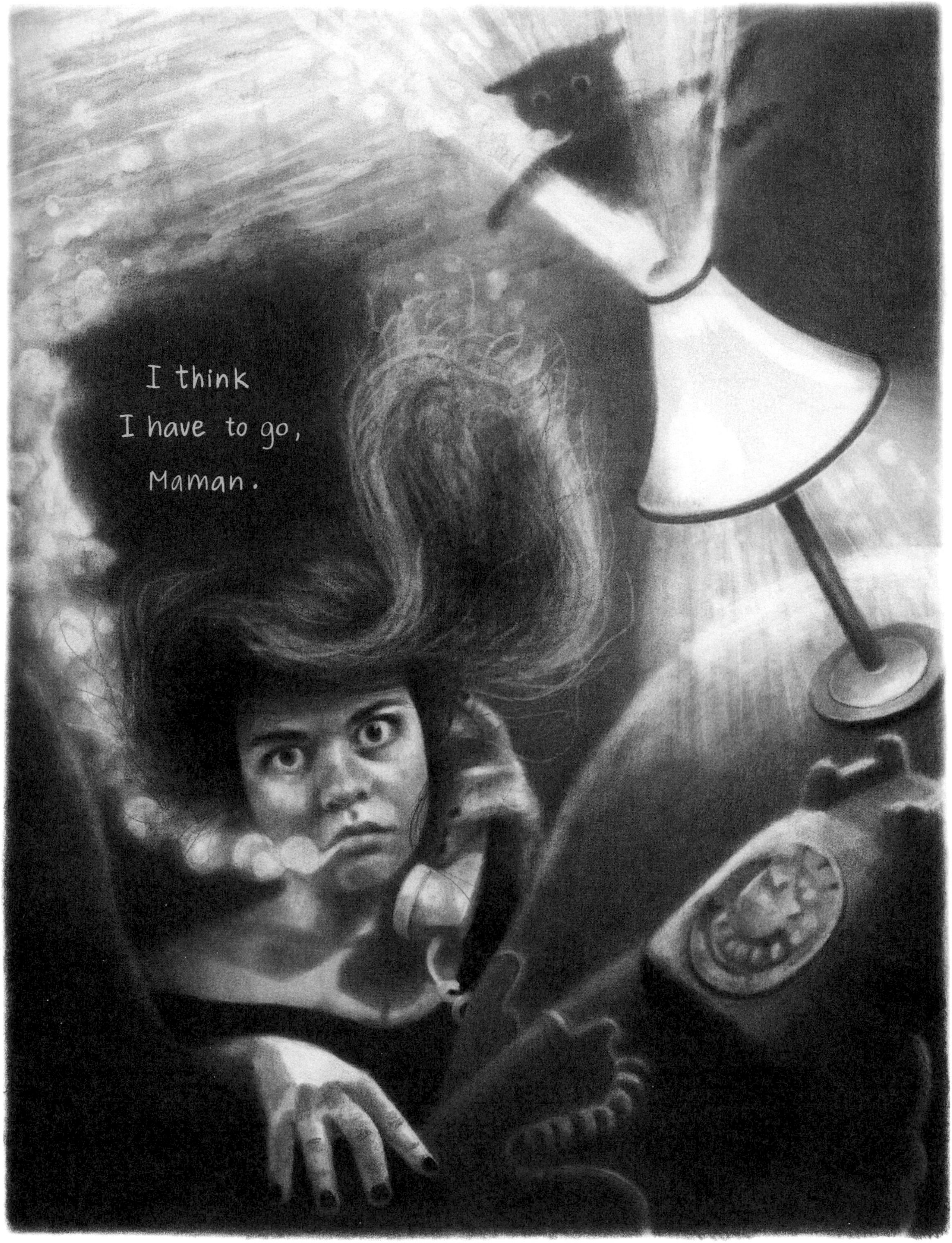
I think
I have to go,
Maman.

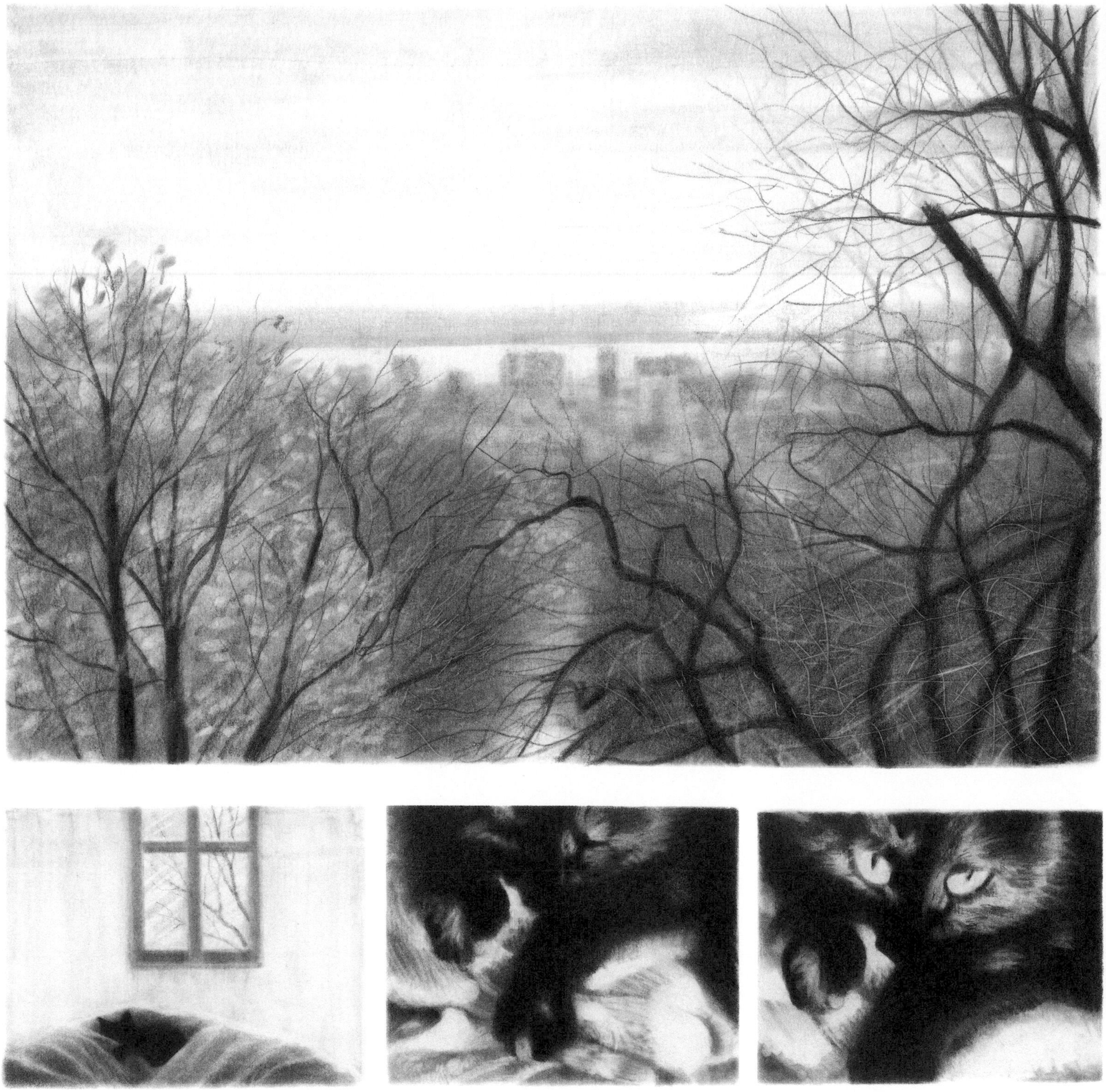

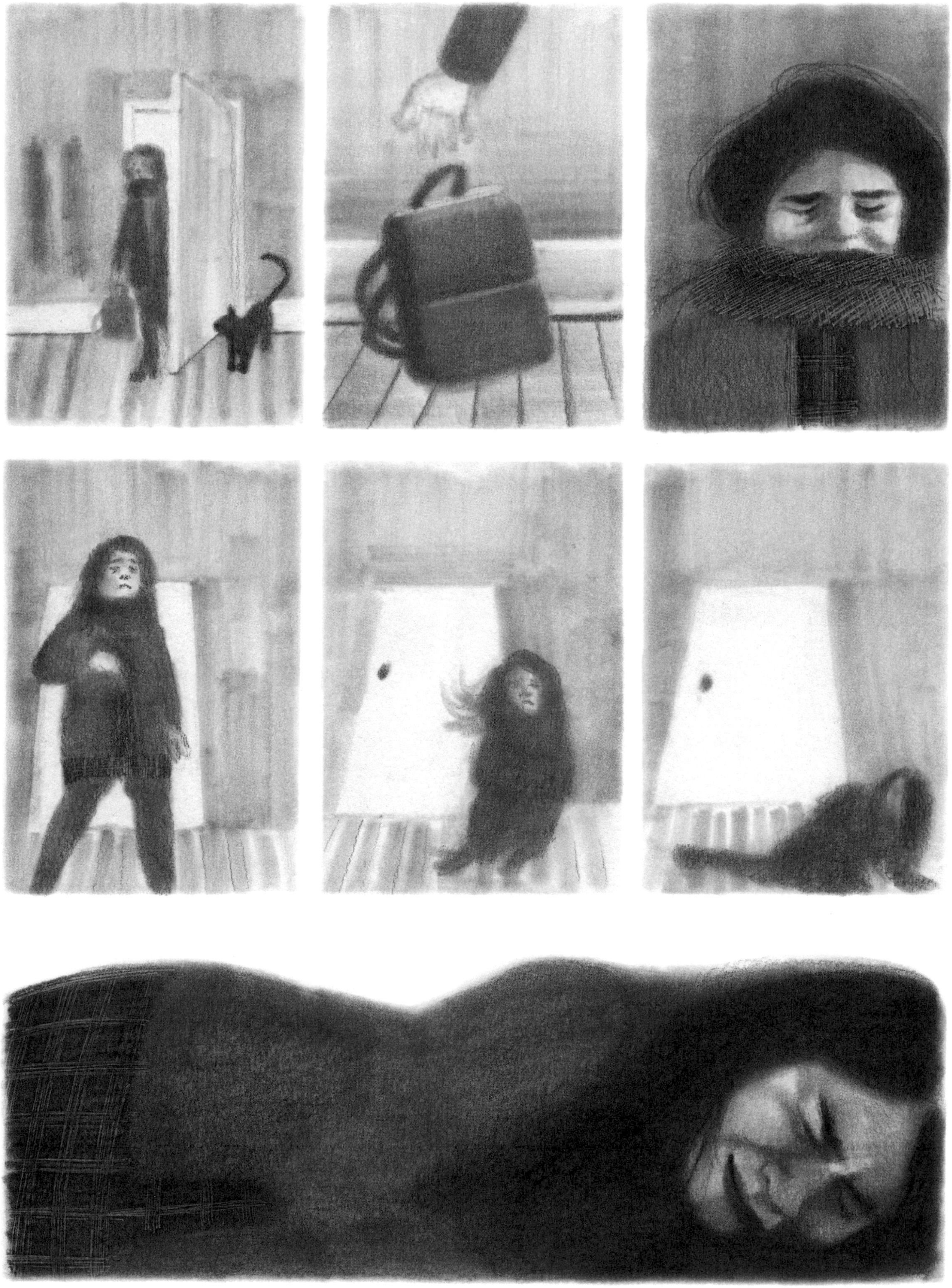

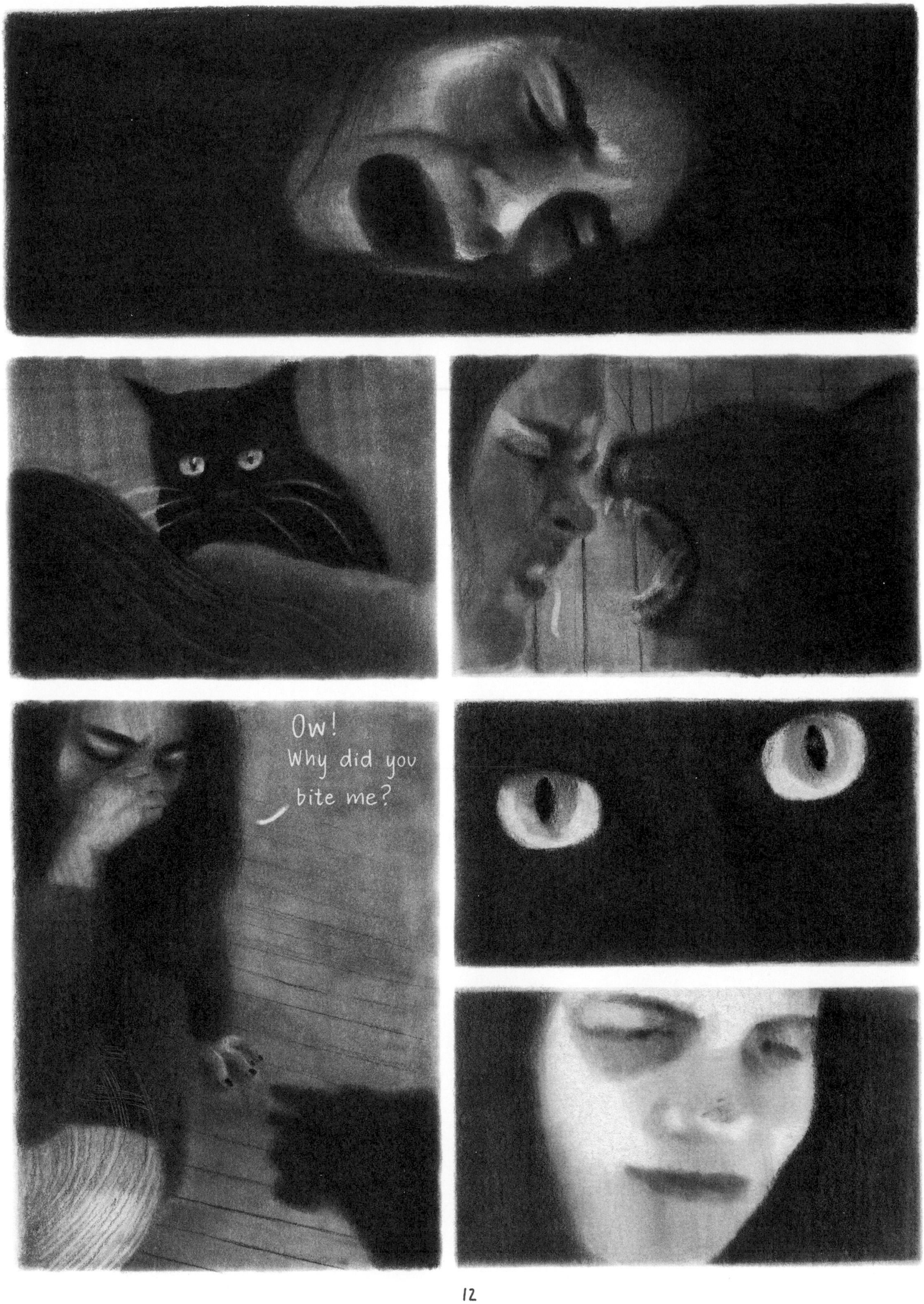
Ow!
Why did you
bite me?

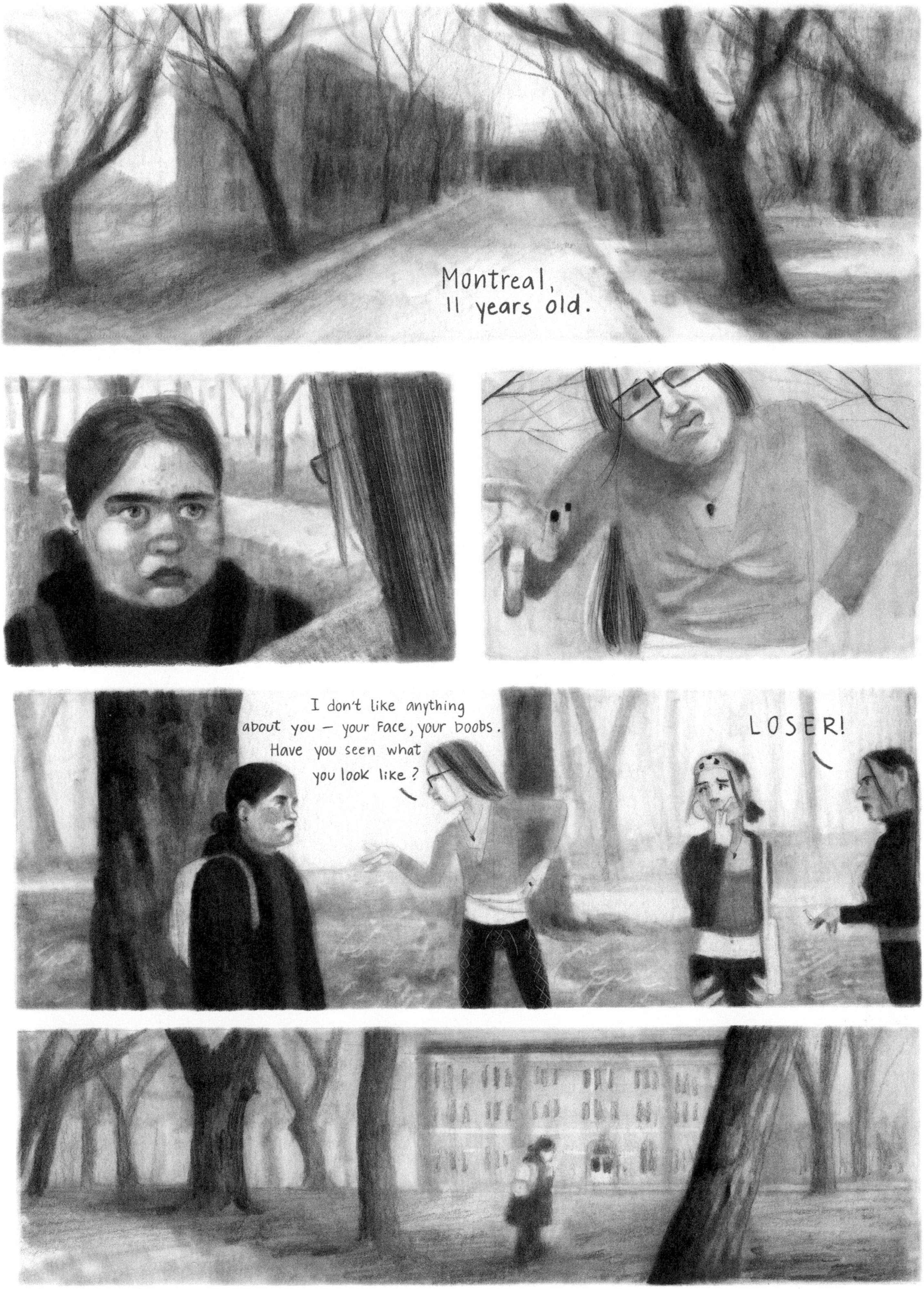

Montreal,
11 years old.
I don't like anything about you – your face, your boobs. Have you seen what you look like?
LOSER!

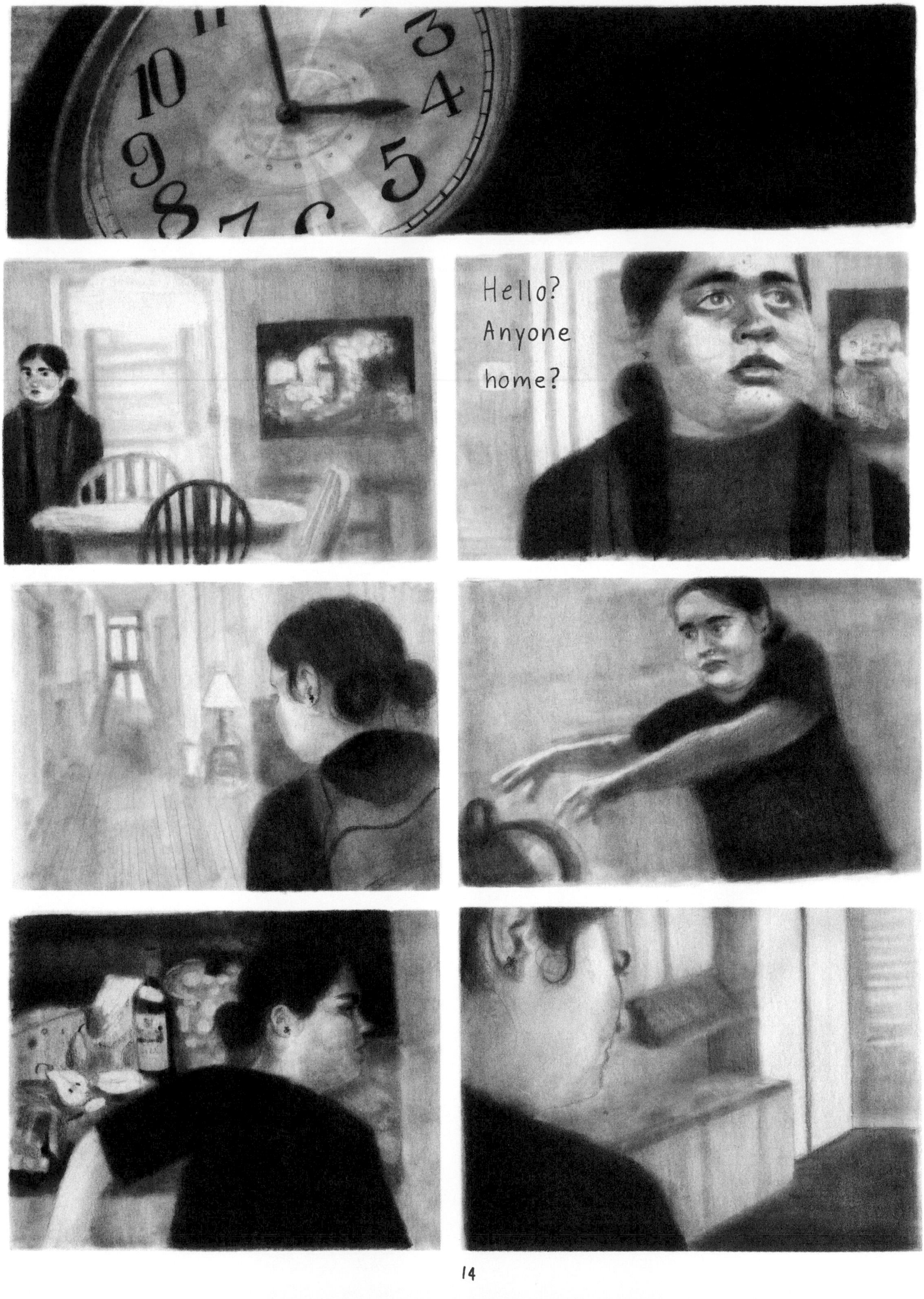
Hello? Anyone home?

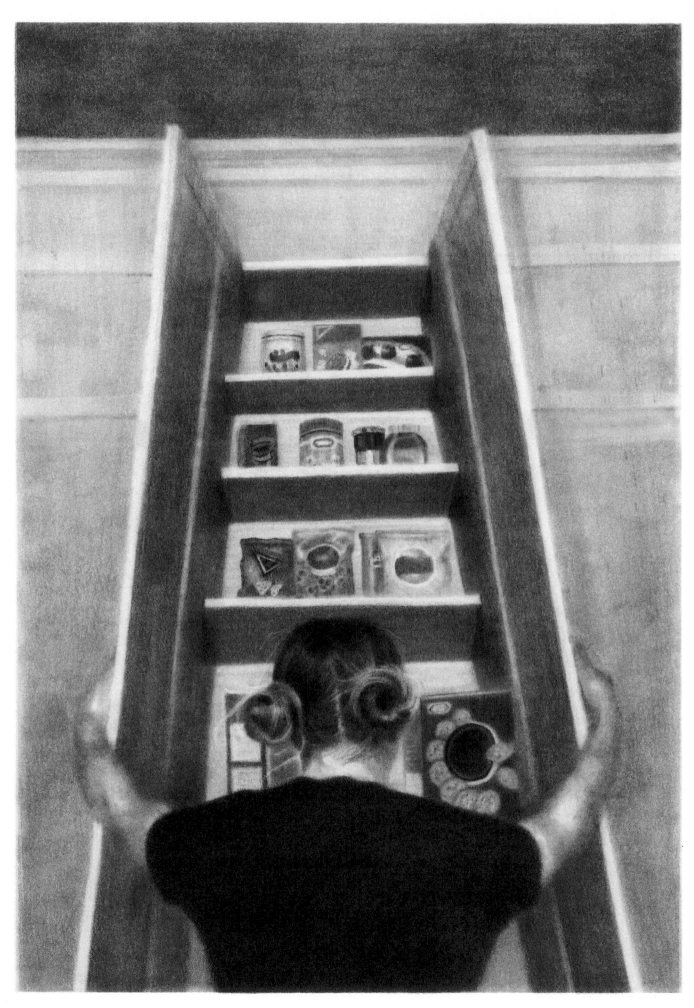

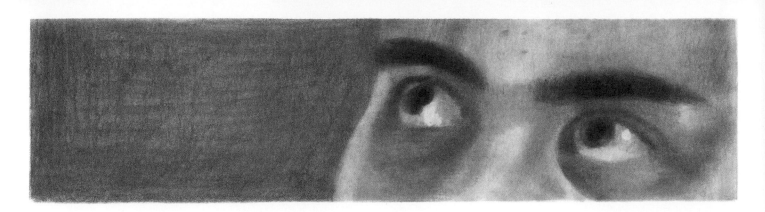

The taste of chips.
I feel relief
when I swallow them
one after another
without stopping.

I hurry.
The others will be
home soon.

The bag is empty.

Fat pig.

FAT!
FAT!
FAT!

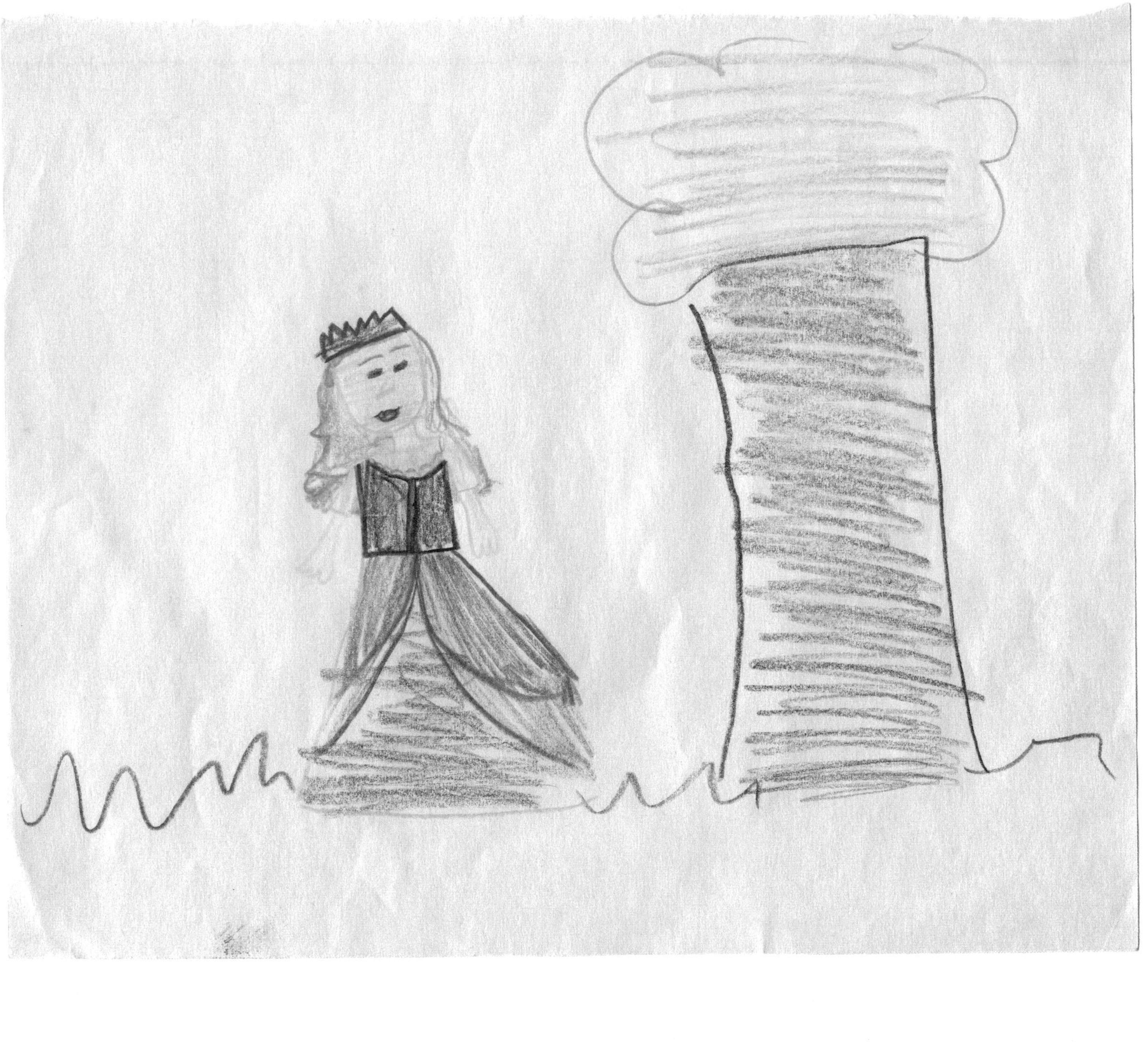

I don't remember the exact moment it took hold of me.

This obsession and fascination.

With princesses.

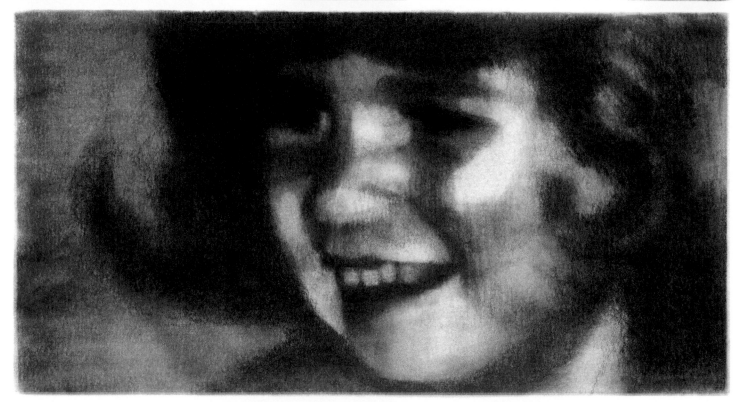

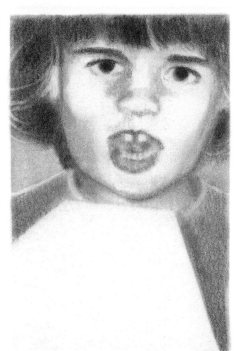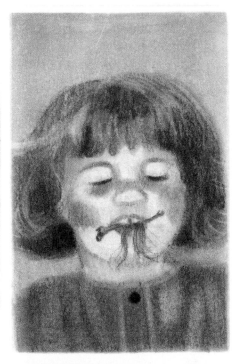

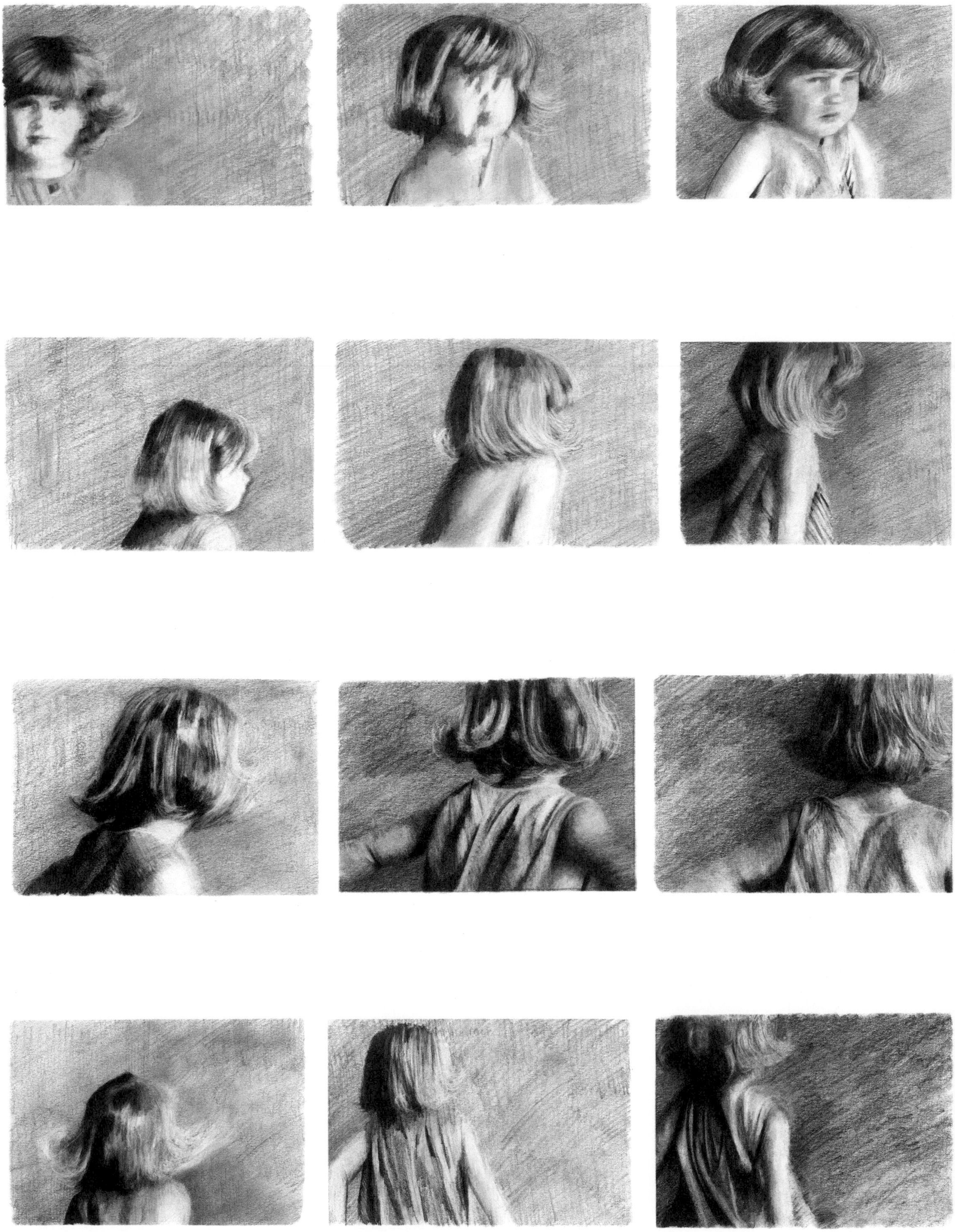

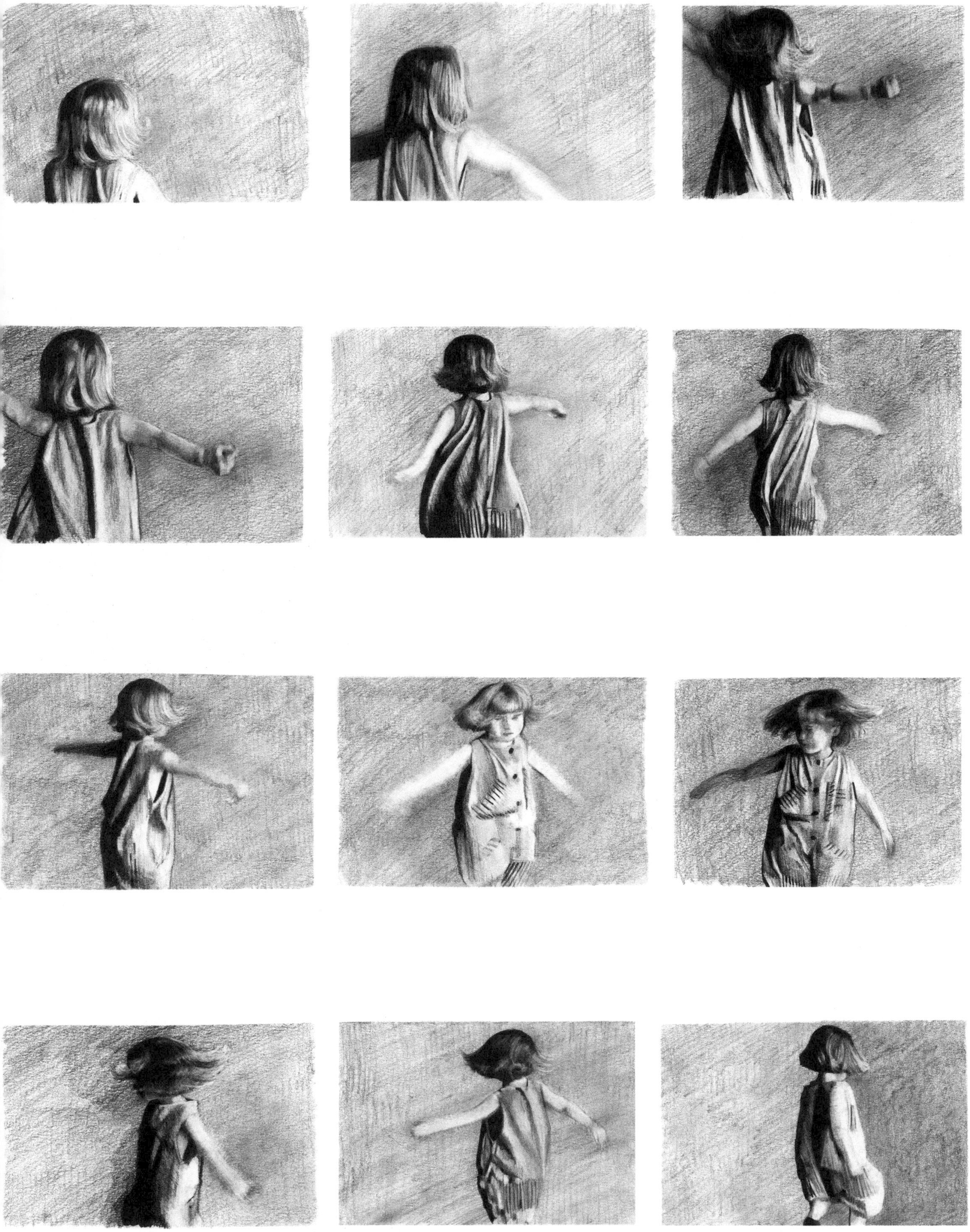

Staz

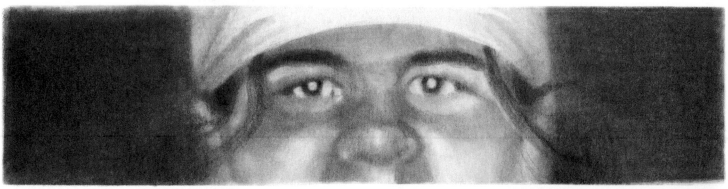

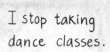
I stop taking dance classes.

I can't keep up anymore, and the costumes are too small.

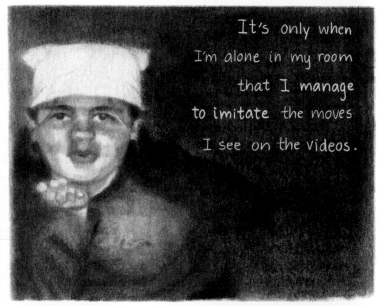
It's only when I'm alone in my room that I manage to imitate the moves I see on the videos.

I put on my stereo and dance in front of my mirror.

I turn into Ashanti, J. Lo or Christina Aguilera.

I'm beautiful.

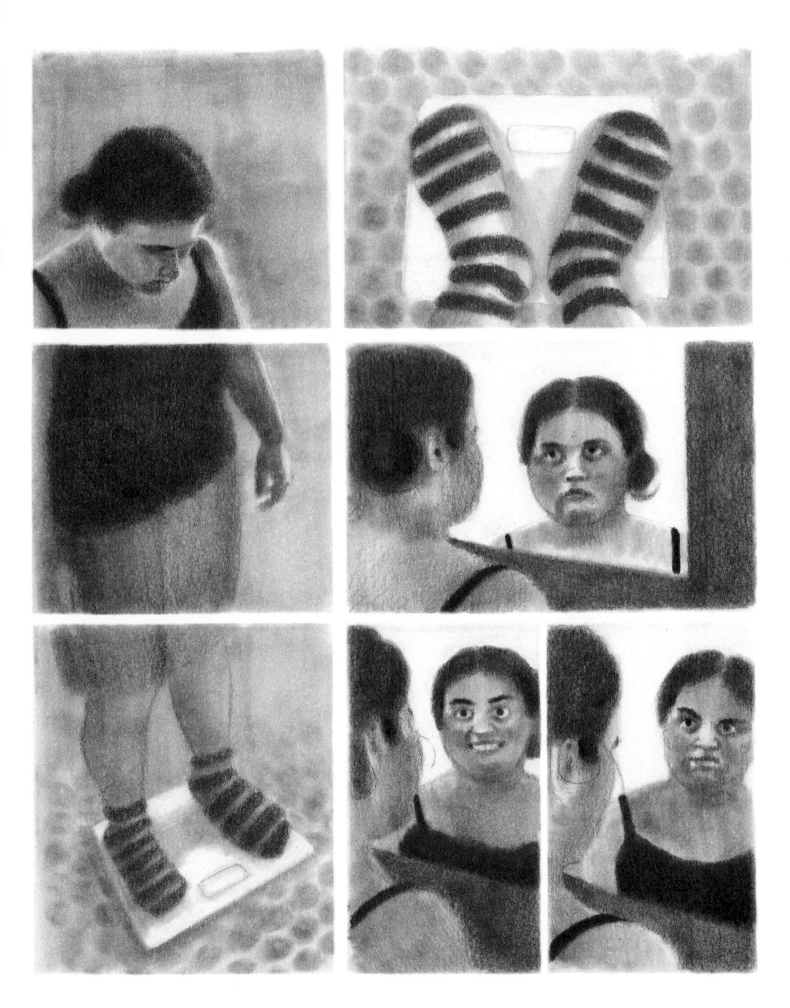

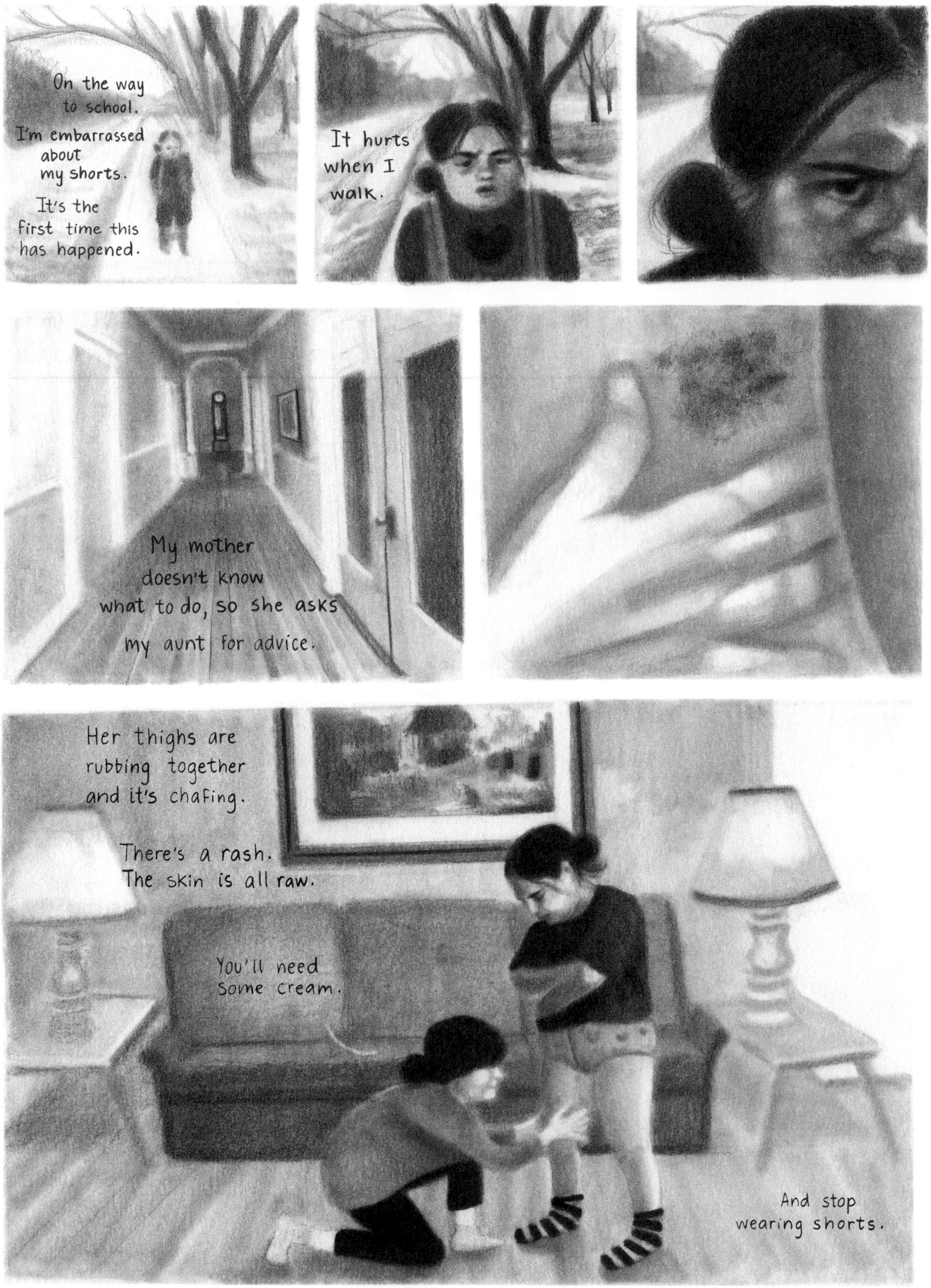
On the way to school.
I'm embarrassed about my shorts.
It's the first time this has happened.
It hurts when I walk.
My mother doesn't know what to do, so she asks my aunt for advice.
Her thighs are rubbing together and it's chafing.
There's a rash. The skin is all raw.
You'll need some cream.
And stop wearing shorts.

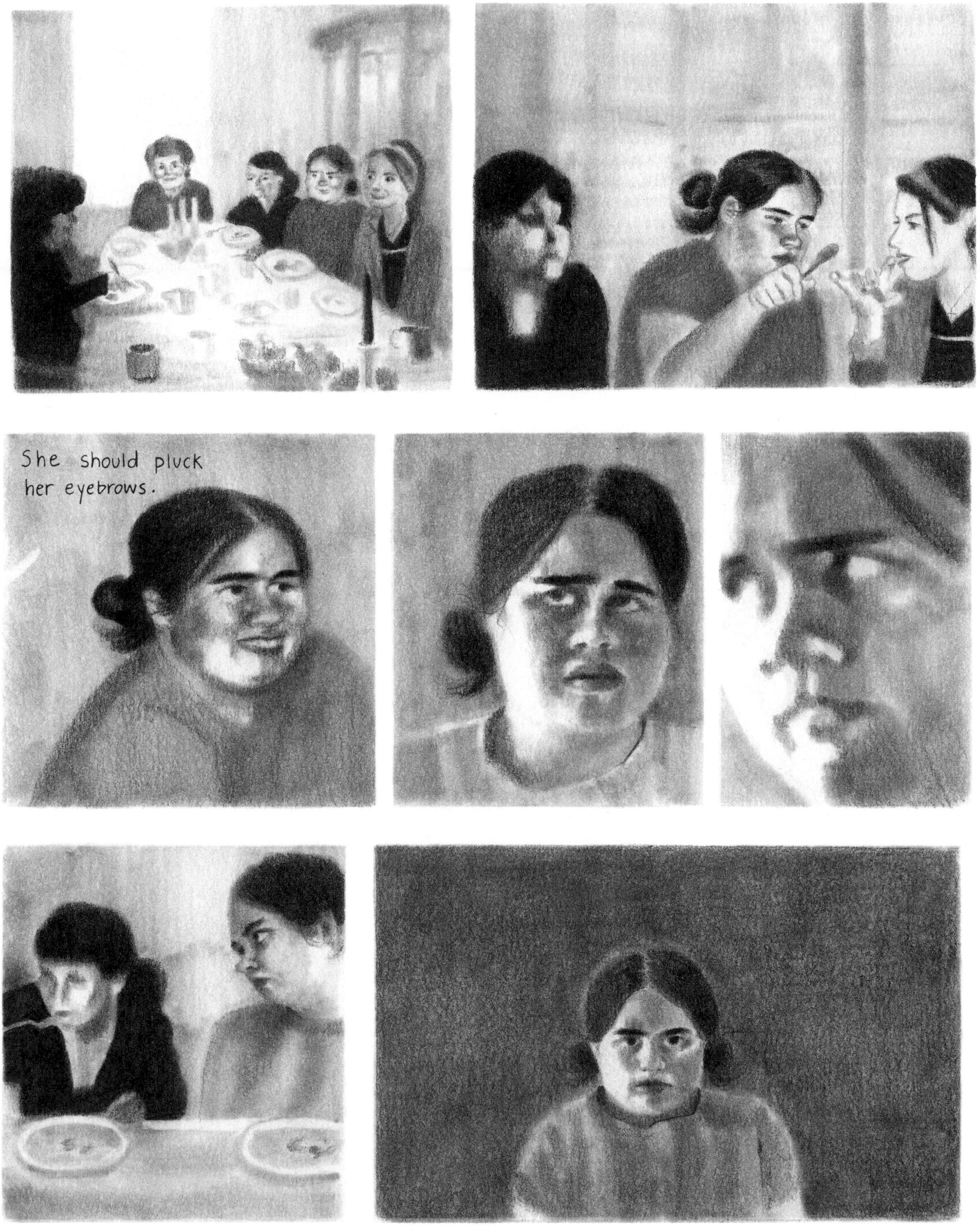
She should pluck her eyebrows.

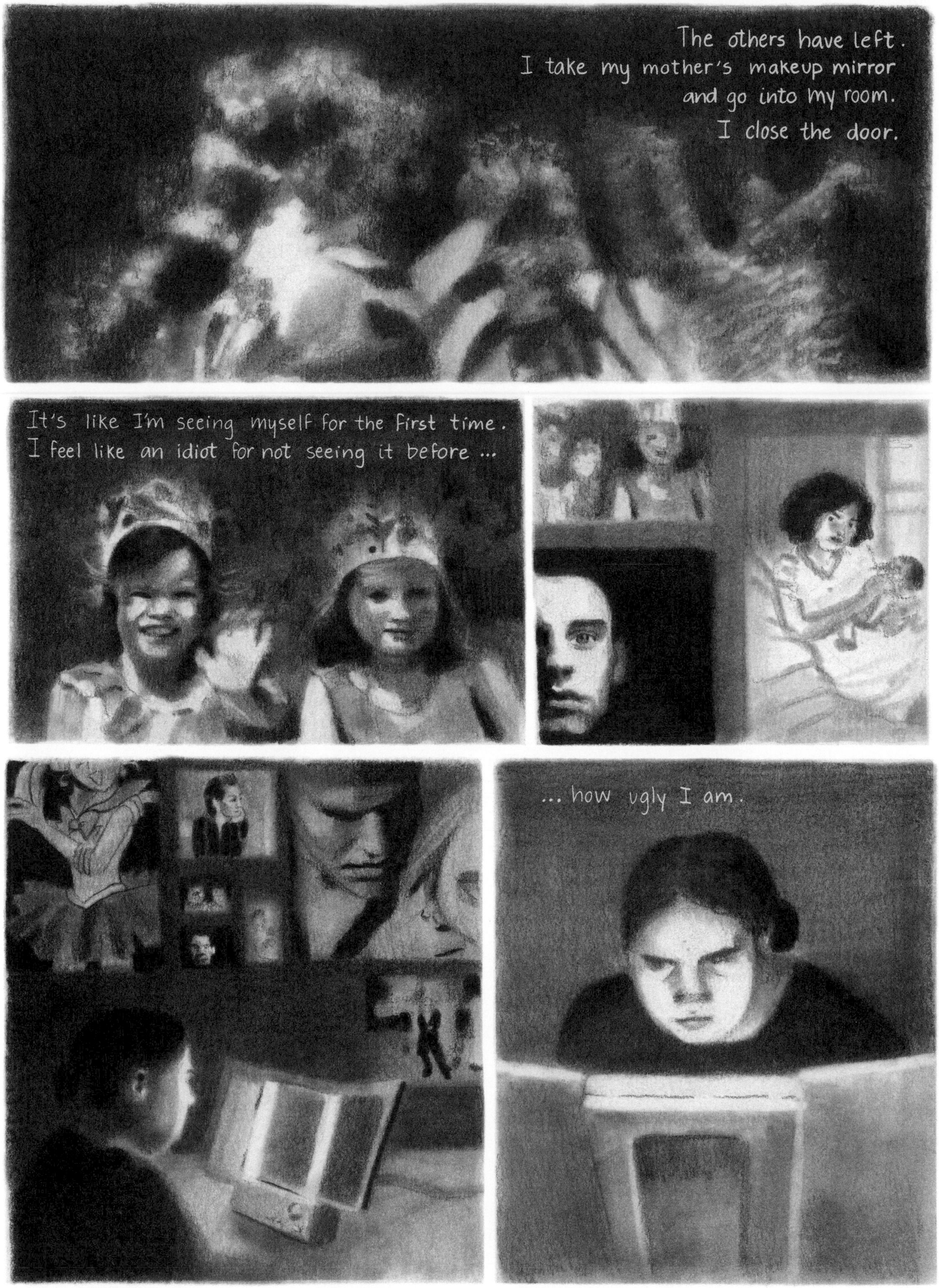
The others have left.
I take my mother's makeup mirror
and go into my room.
I close the door.
It's like I'm seeing myself for the first time.
I feel like an idiot for not seeing it before ...
... how ugly I am.

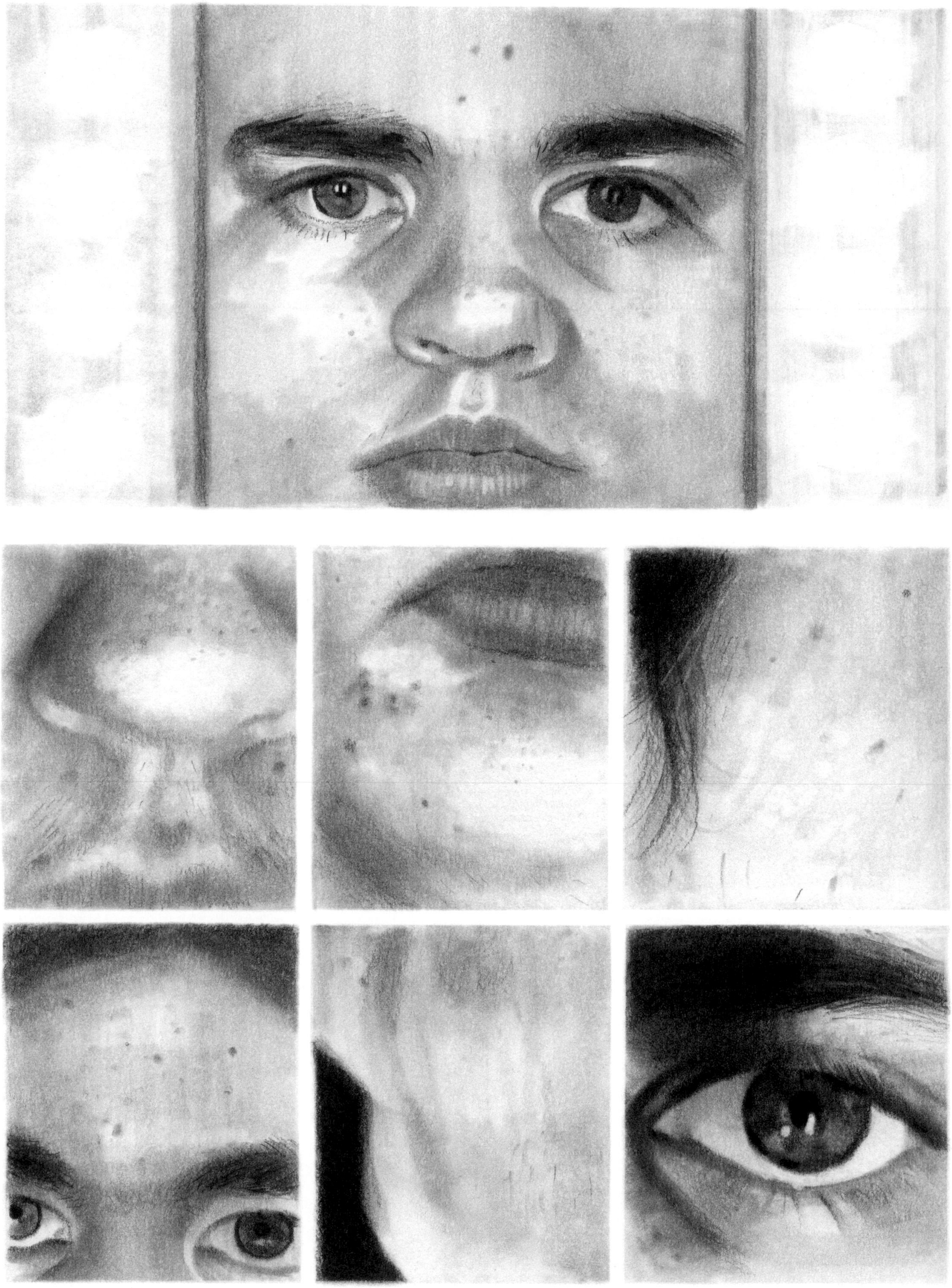

Each day I focus on finding fault with my body, one piece at a time.

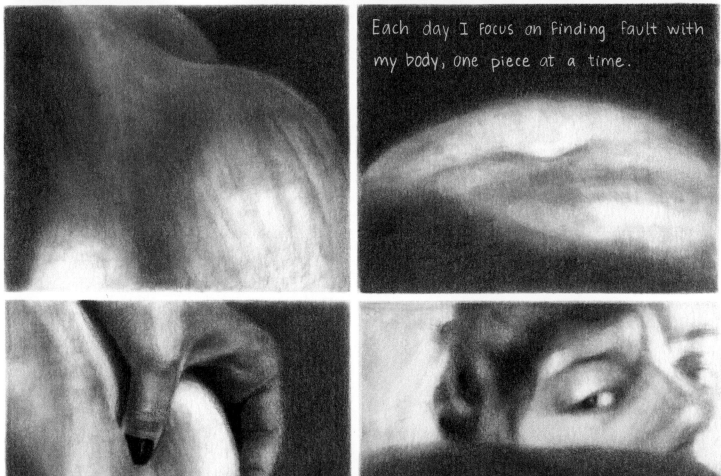

I'm good at it.

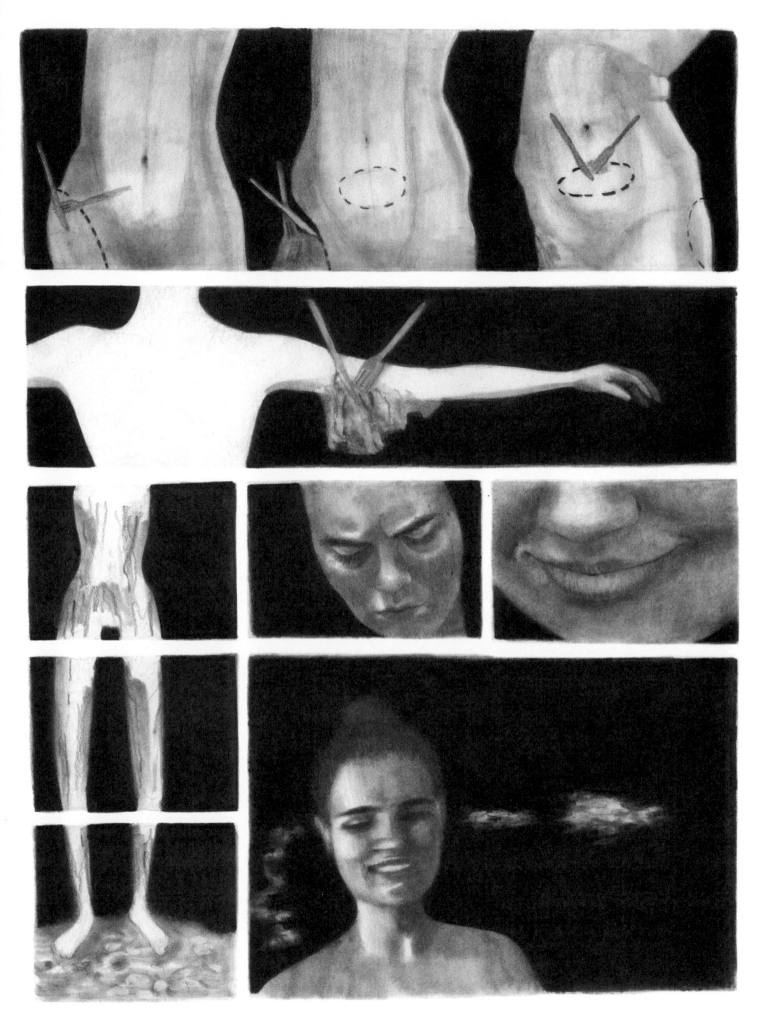

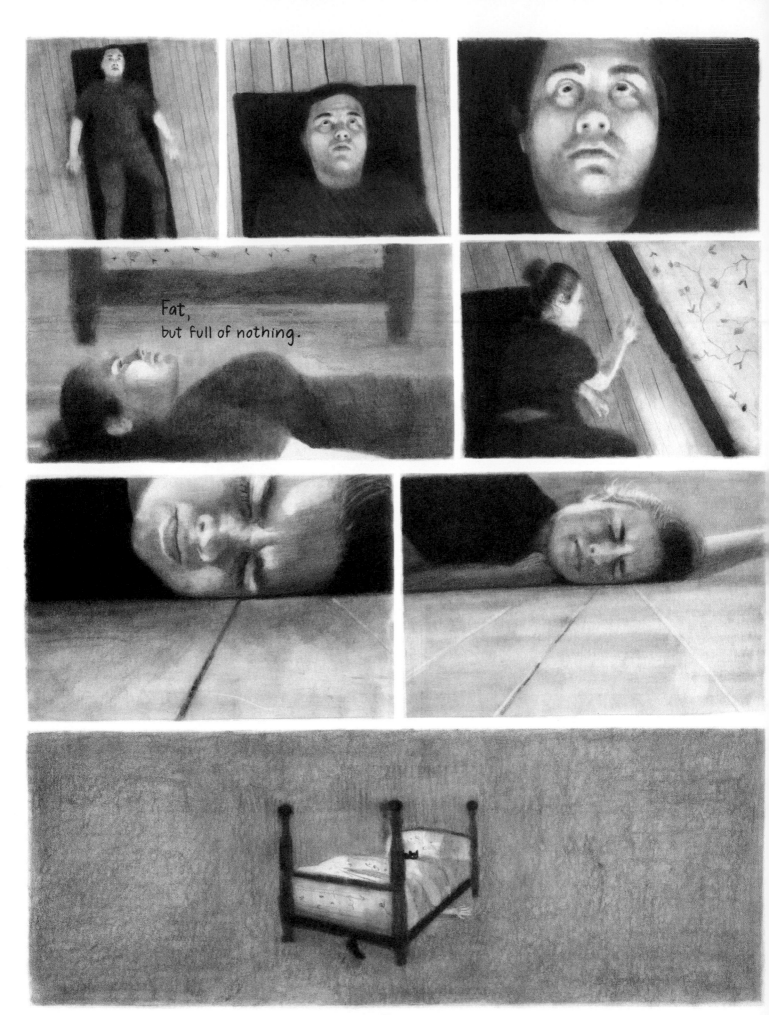

Fat,
but full of nothing.

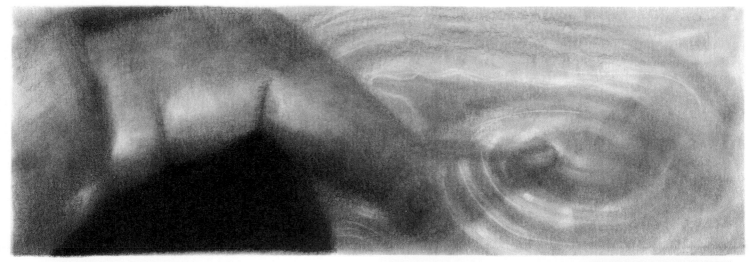

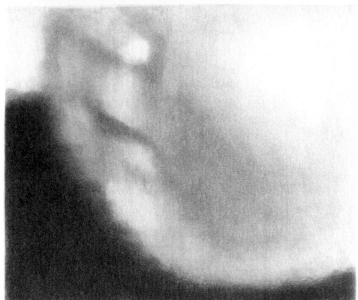

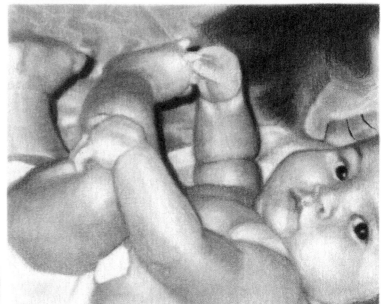

Marie-Noëlle Hébert, born June 18, 1990. A beautiful big baby.

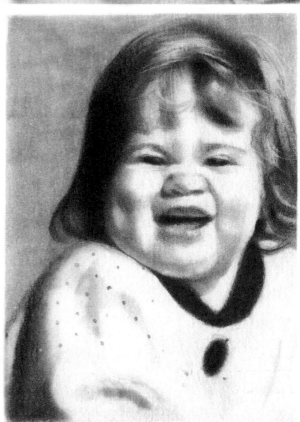

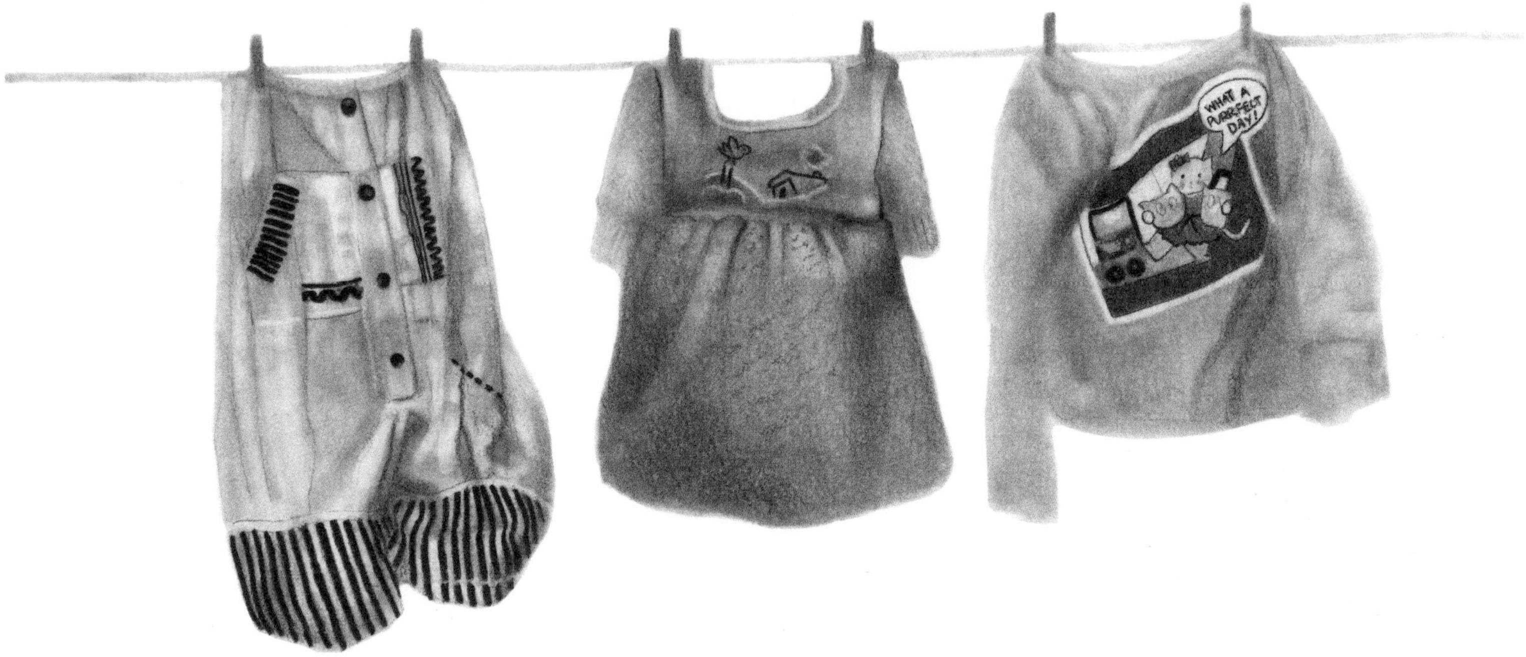
WHAT A PURR-FECT DAY!

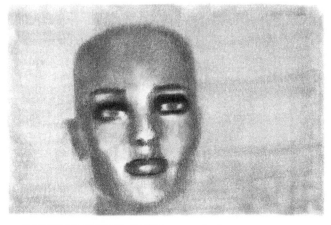

8 years old.
My mother takes me shopping
because my clothes
don't fit anymore.
But I hate shopping.

Come on,
let's go.

She said we would find some
nice clothes at Sears.

So it won't look
as though I'm
wearing clothes
from the women's
department.

What would you
like to try on?

Nothing.
It's all
ugly.

So, how do you feel in it?

I look like an old lady.

Look, try this on first.

It won't do up.

And they're too tight.

I'll hem it for you.

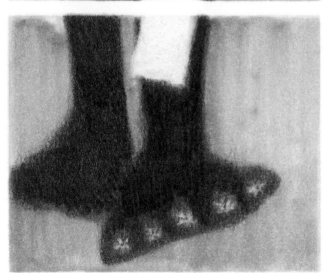

I'm fat.

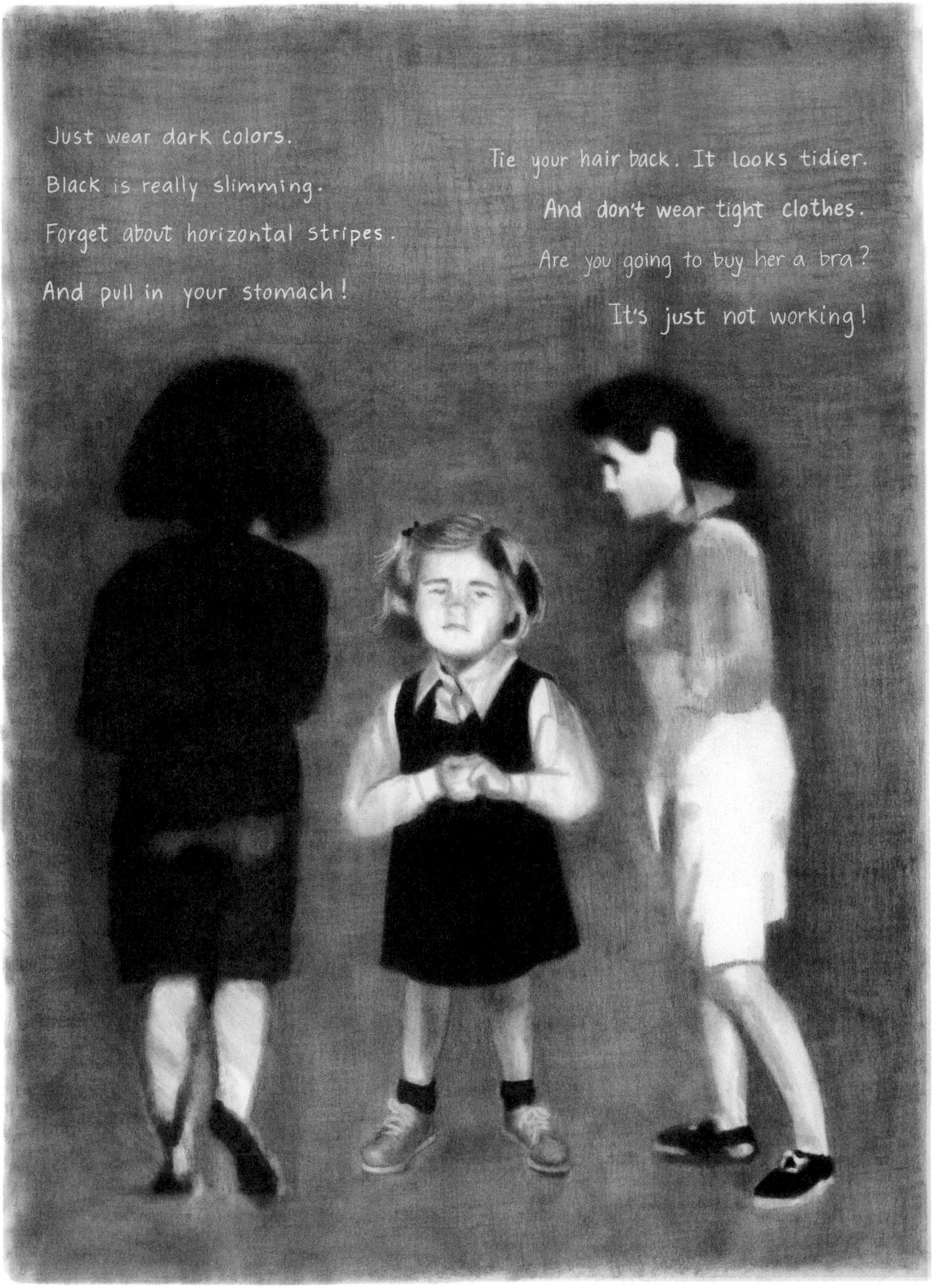
Just wear dark colors.
Black is really slimming.
Forget about horizontal stripes.
And pull in your stomach!
Tie your hair back. It looks tidier.
And don't wear tight clothes.
Are you going to buy her a bra?
It's just not working!

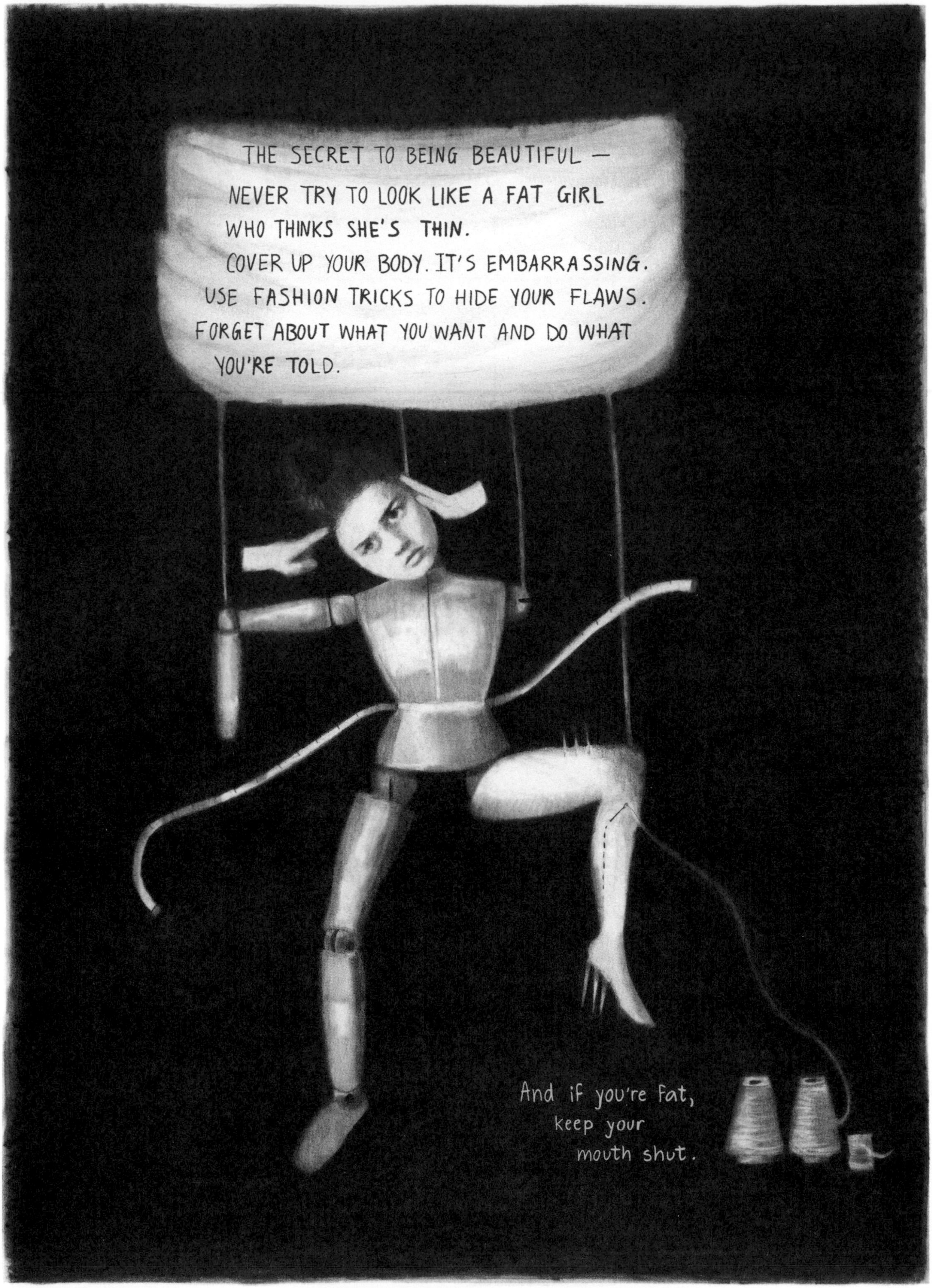
THE SECRET TO BEING BEAUTIFUL —
NEVER TRY TO LOOK LIKE A FAT GIRL
WHO THINKS SHE'S THIN.
COVER UP YOUR BODY. IT'S EMBARRASSING.
USE FASHION TRICKS TO HIDE YOUR FLAWS.
FORGET ABOUT WHAT YOU WANT AND DO WHAT
YOU'RE TOLD.
And if you're fat,
keep your
mouth shut.

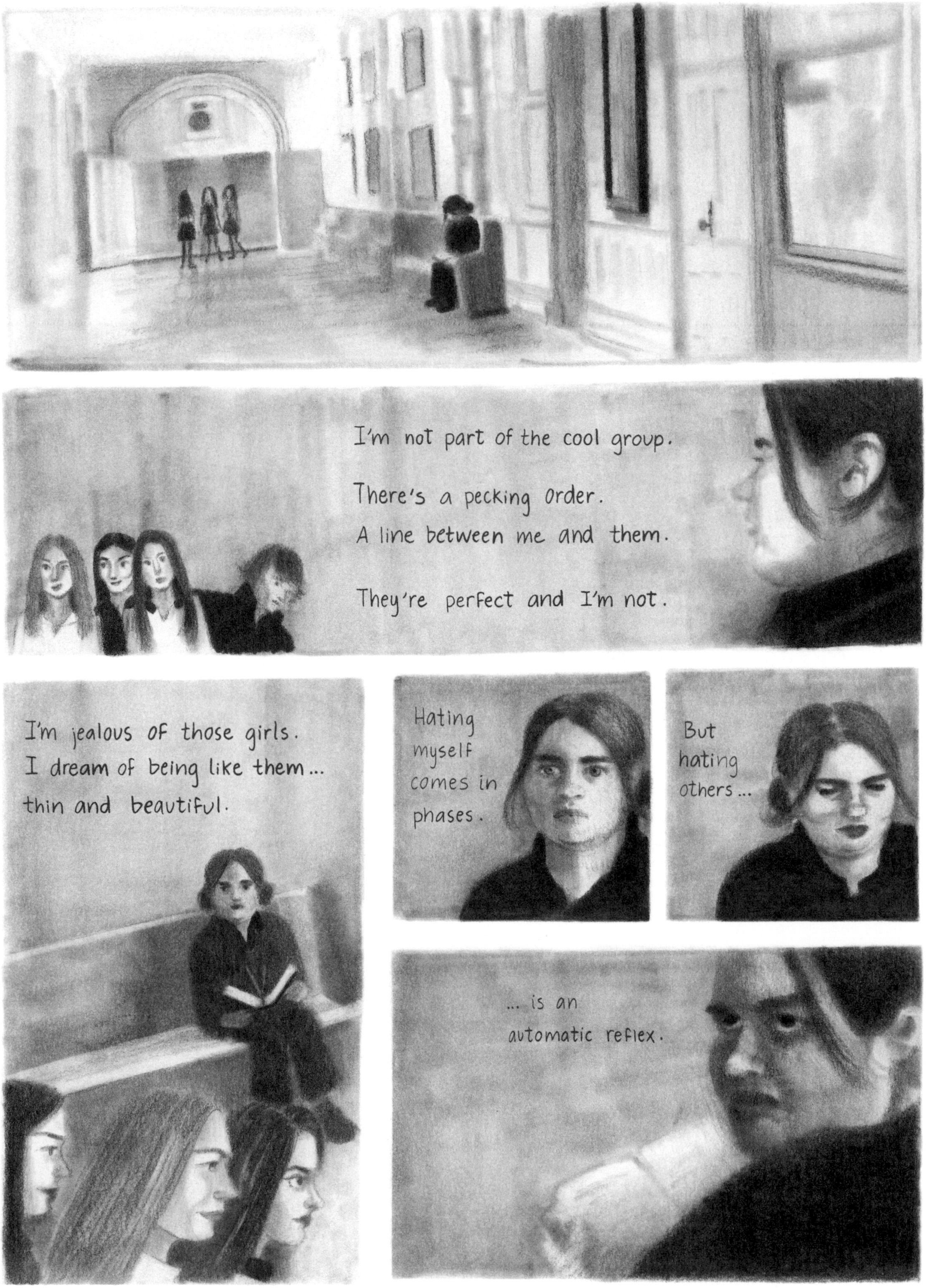
I'm not part of the cool group.
There's a pecking order.
A line between me and them.
They're perfect and I'm not.
I'm jealous of those girls.
I dream of being like them...
thin and beautiful.
Hating myself comes in phases.
But hating others...
... is an automatic reflex.

Shit shit shit!

i'm fed up with no one really
        listening to me.
    I just feel like a loser.
I hate myself.
    Big and Fat.

Stress   pounds
        Fat   Hating myself

I want to lose weight!
I was okay a month ago, but then
everything fell apart!

It pisses me off.

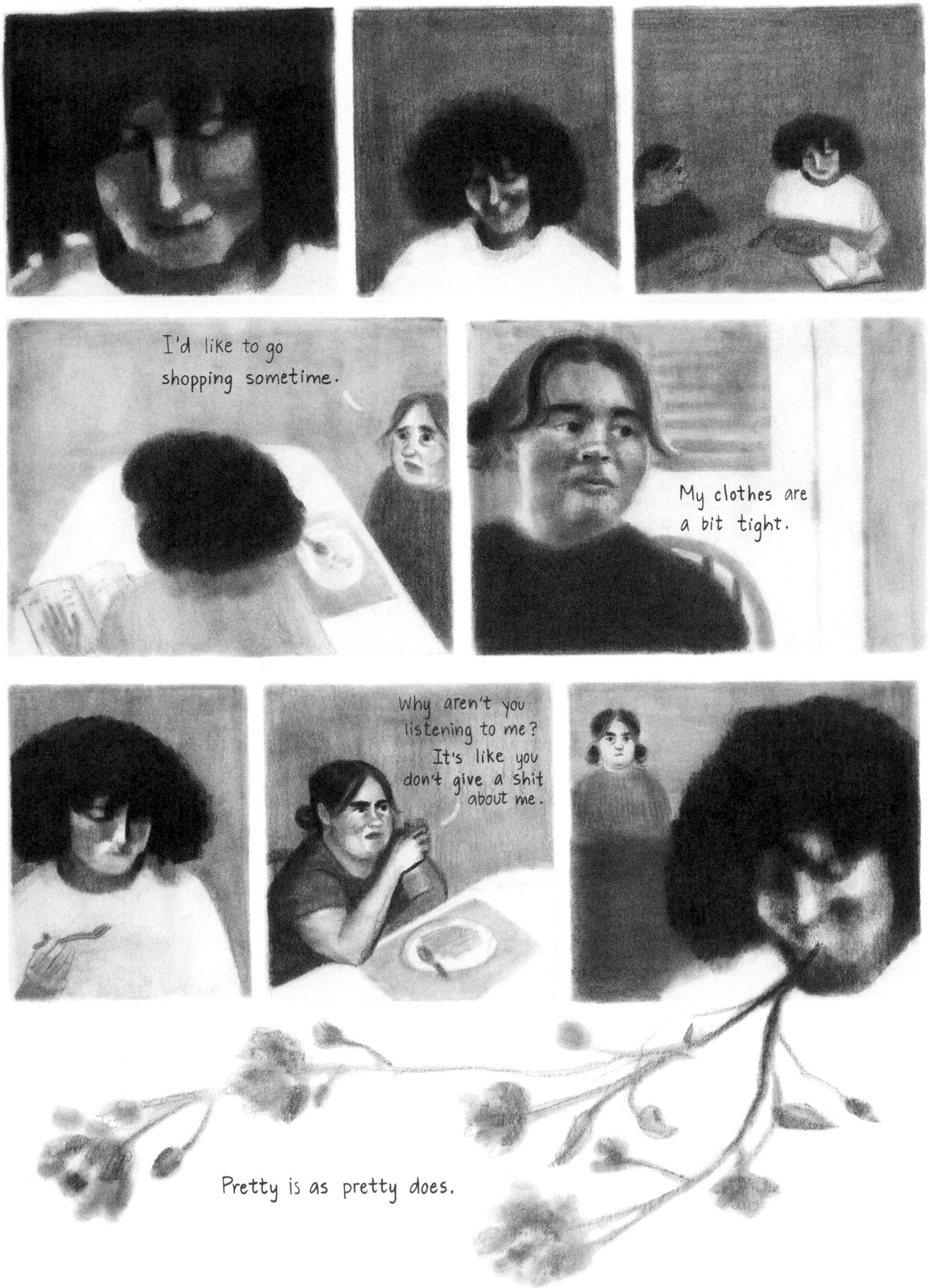
I'd like to go shopping sometime.
My clothes are a bit tight.
Why aren't you listening to me? It's like you don't give a shit about me.
Pretty is as pretty does.

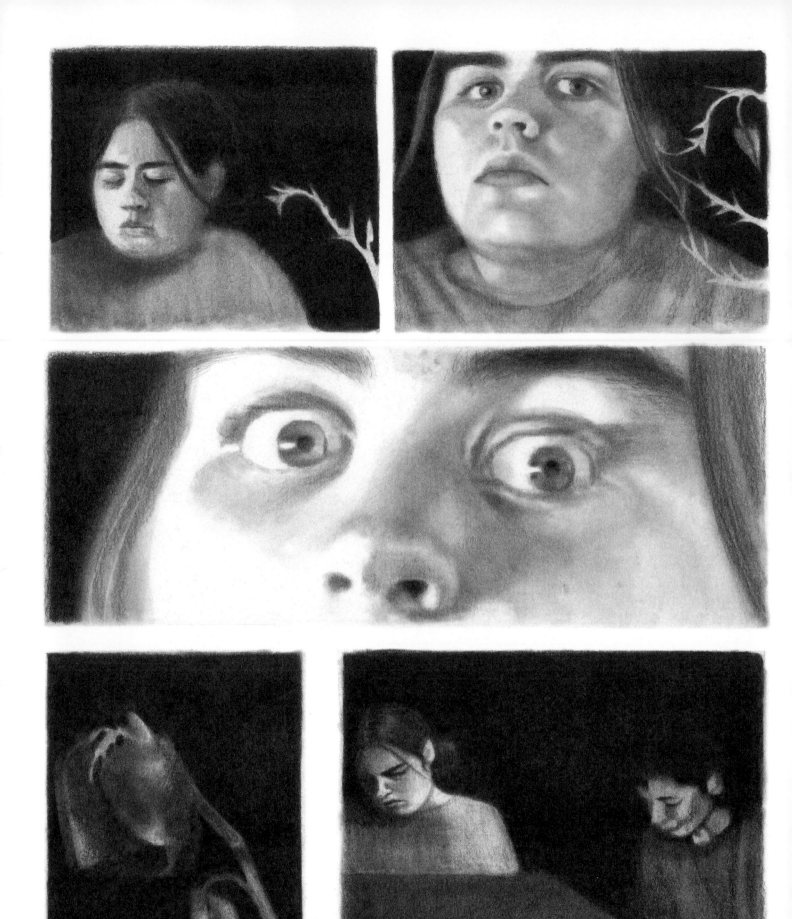

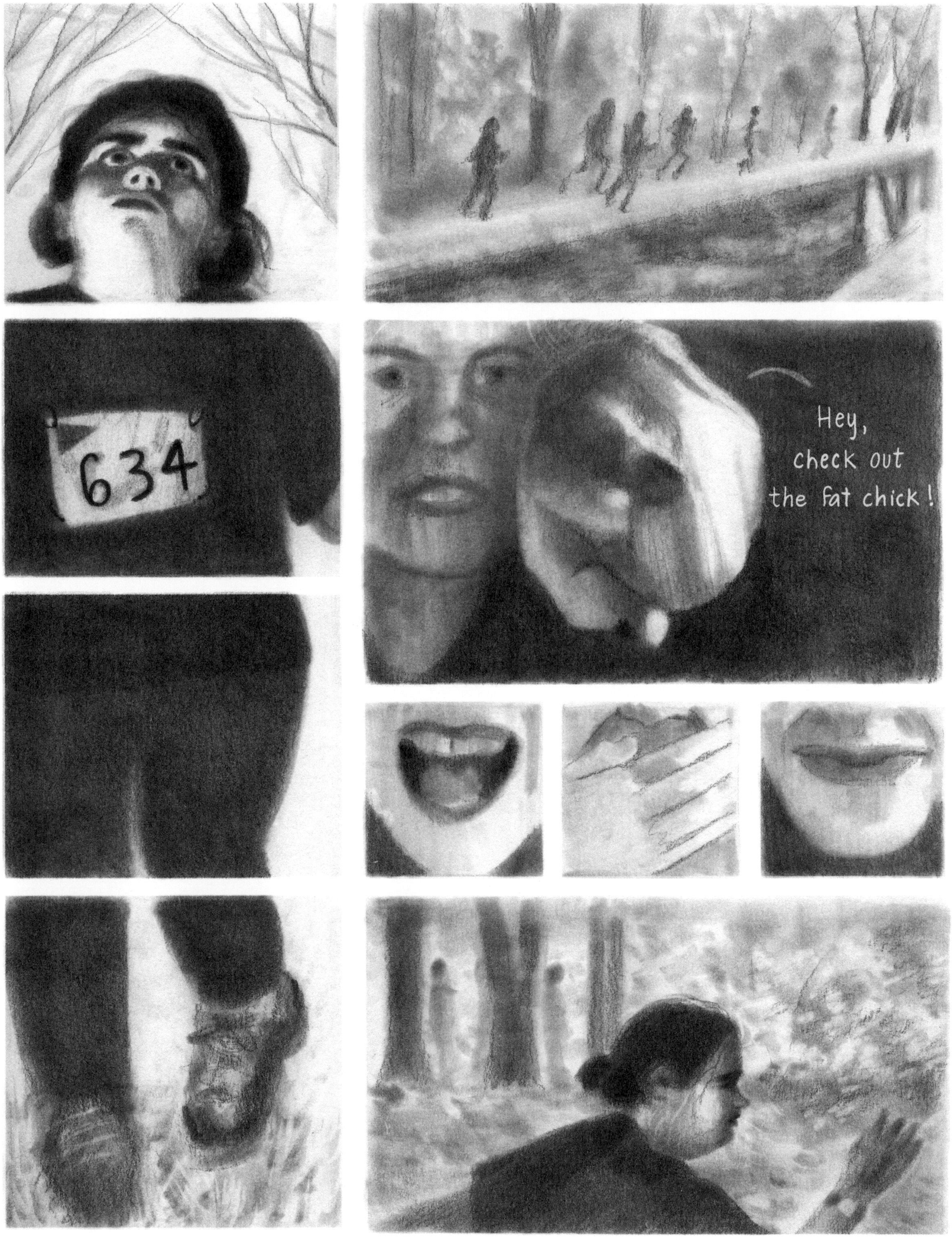
634
Hey, check out the fat chick!

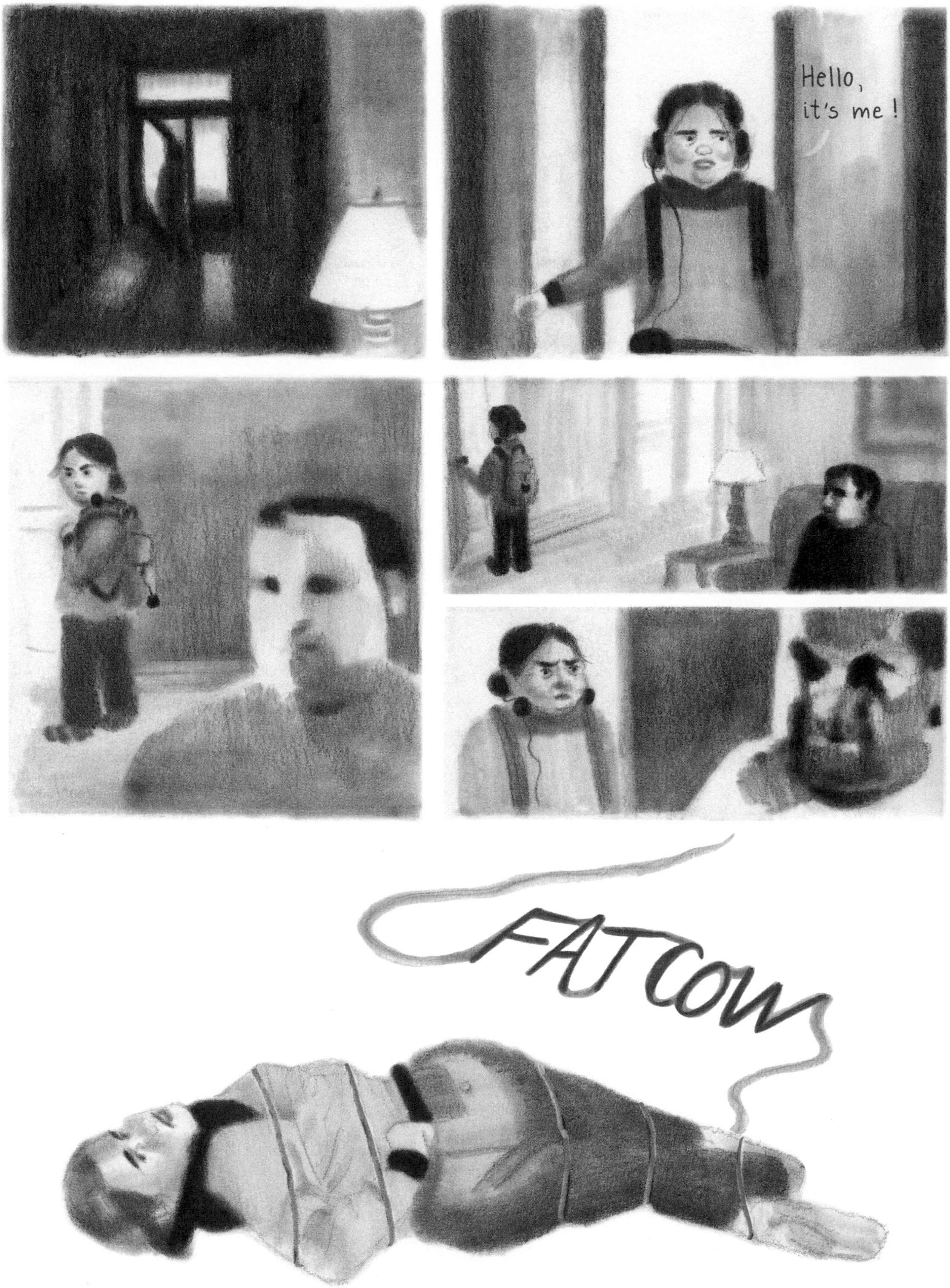
Hello,
it's me!
FAT COW

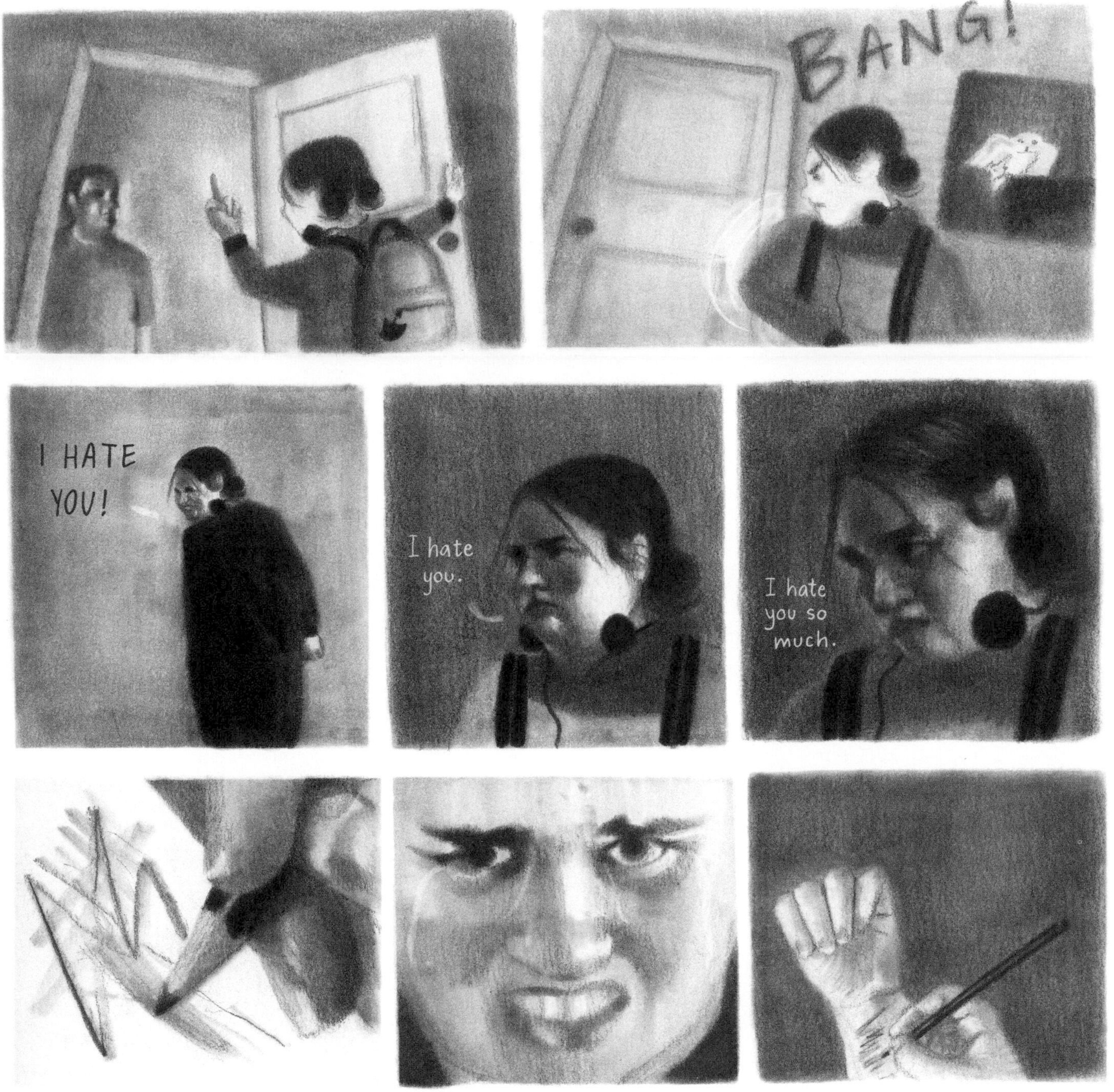
BANG!
I HATE YOU!
I hate you.
I hate you so much.
I HATE ME
I HATE ME
I HATE ME

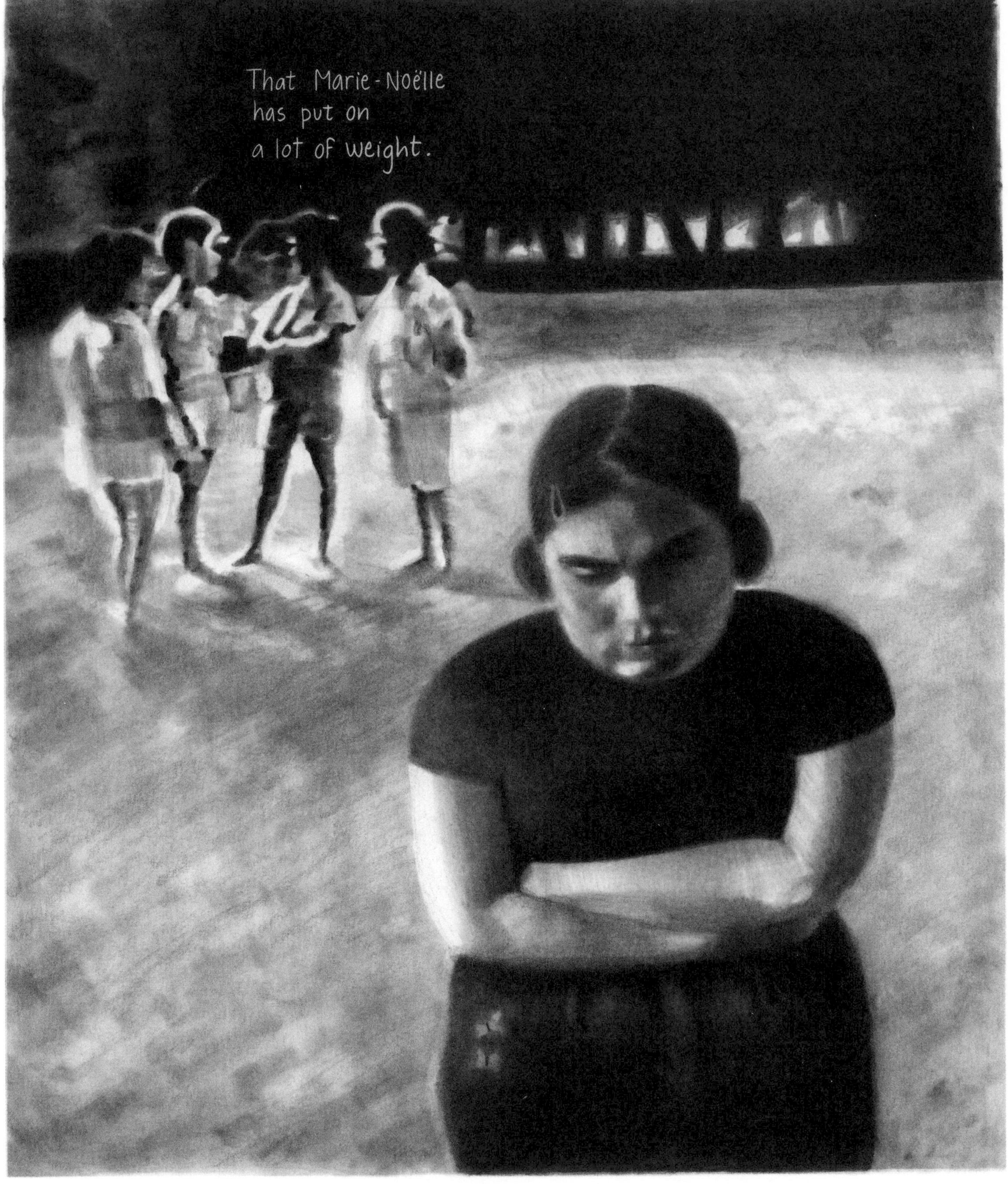
That Marie-Noëlle has put on a lot of weight.

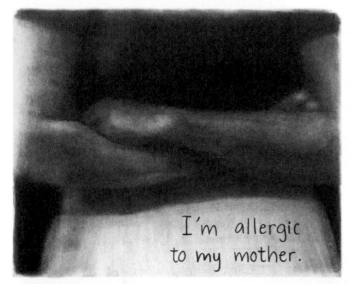

I'm allergic
to my mother.

All this lovey-dovey stuff.
I can't stand it.

Hello,
sweetie!

Hi.

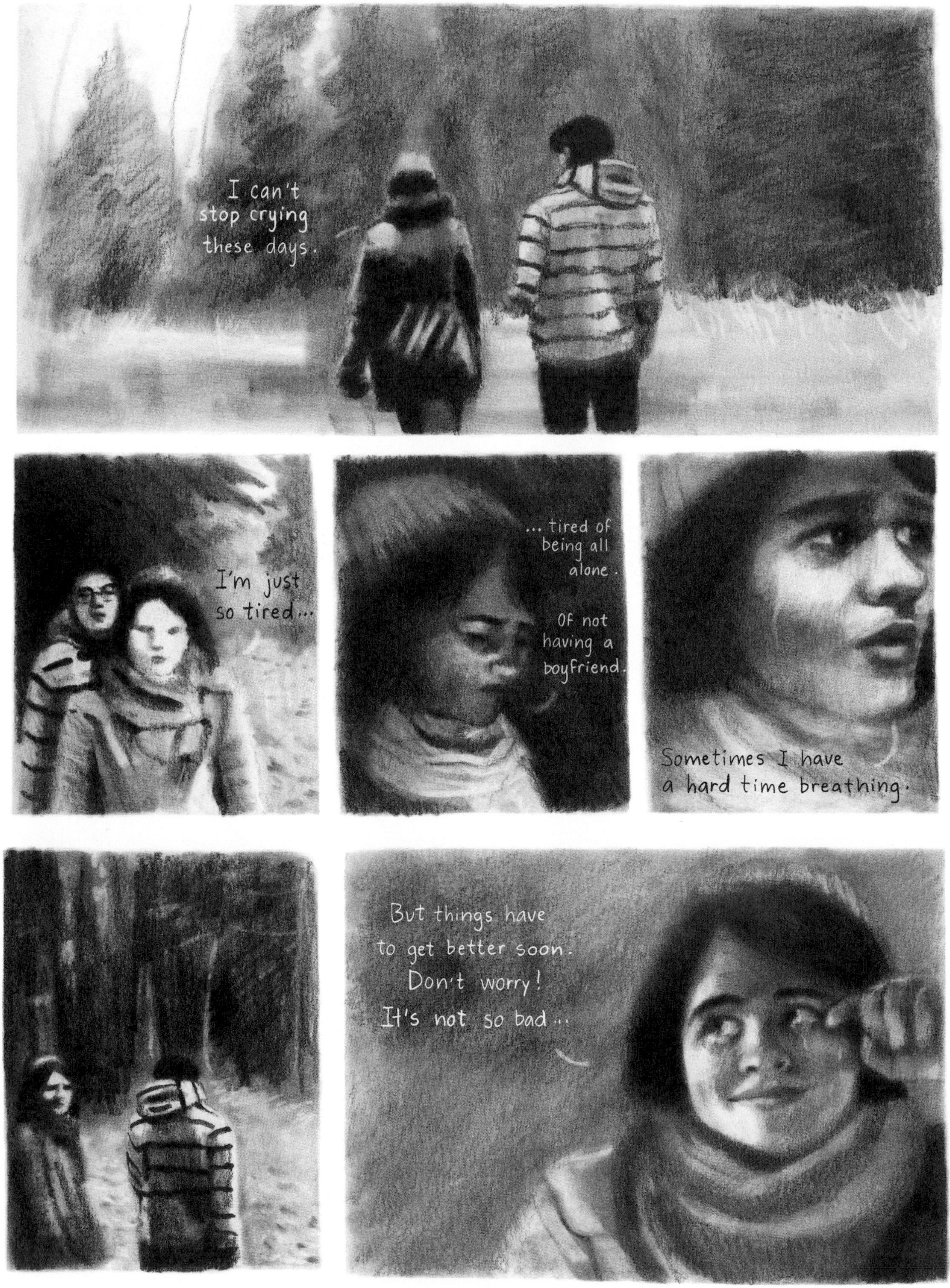
I can't stop crying these days.
I'm just so tired...
... tired of being all alone.
Of not having a boyfriend.
Sometimes I have a hard time breathing.
But things have to get better soon. Don't worry! It's not so bad...

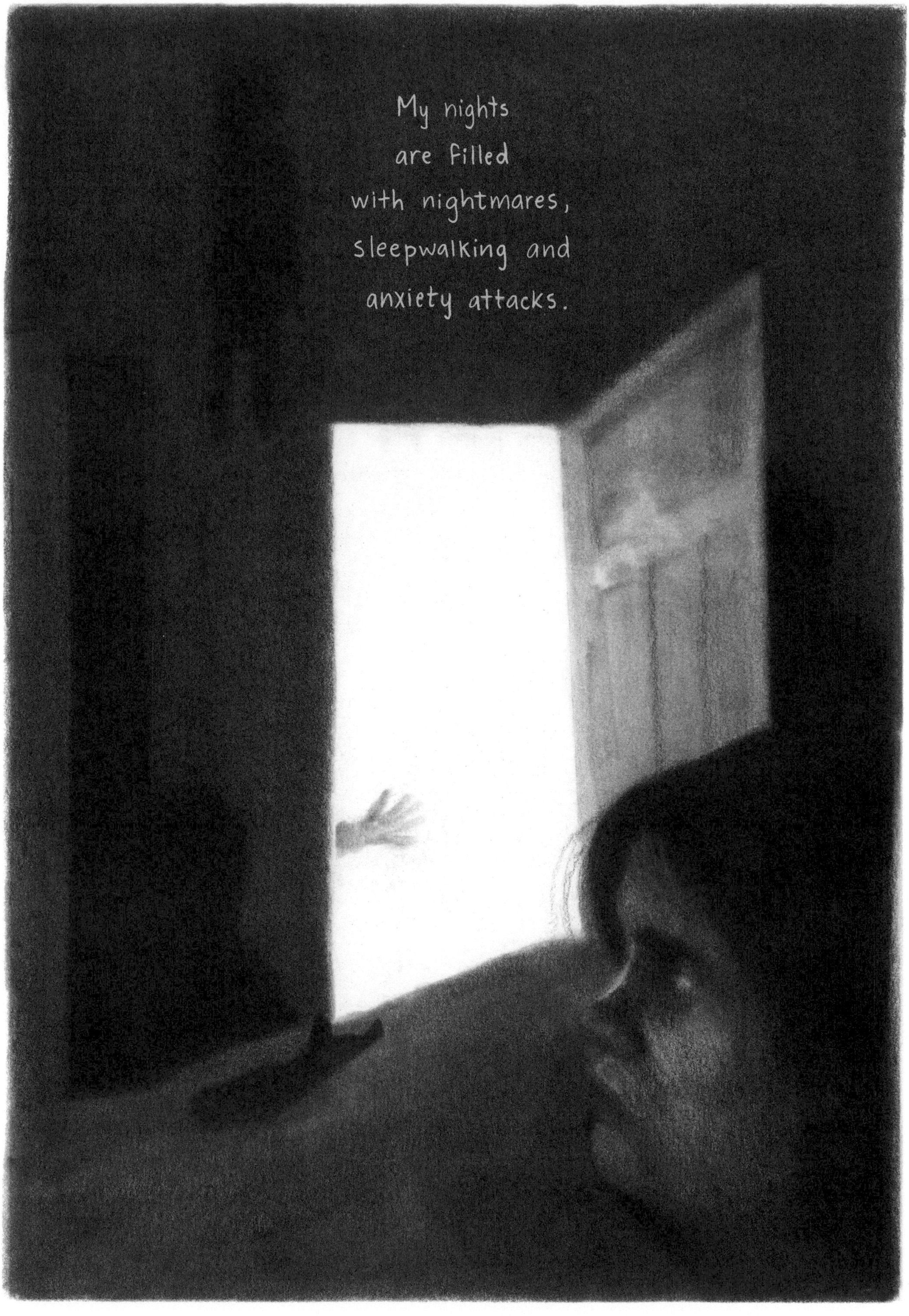
My nights
are filled
with nightmares,
sleepwalking and
anxiety attacks.

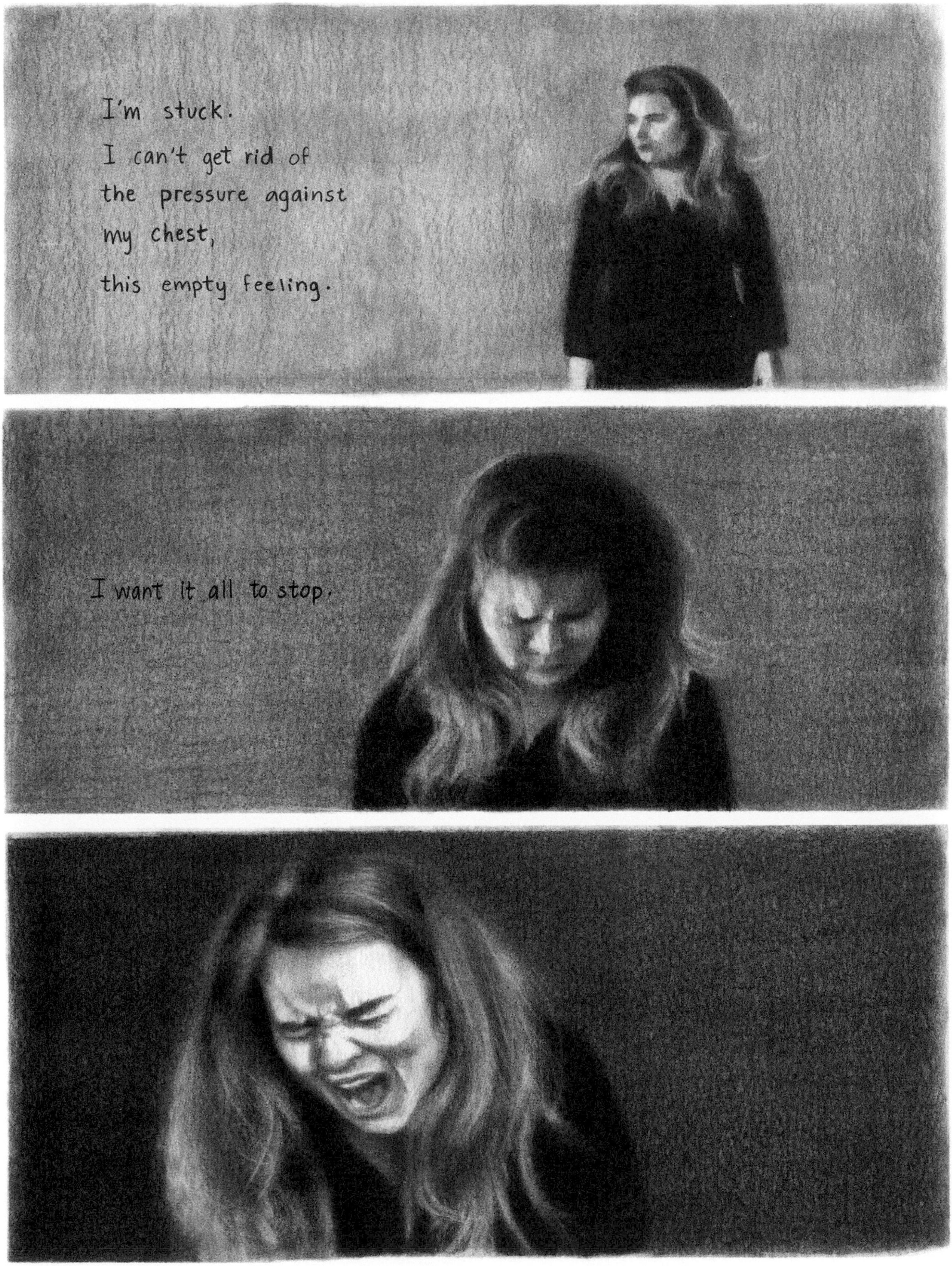
I'm stuck.
I can't get rid of the pressure against my chest,
this empty feeling.
I want it all to stop.

  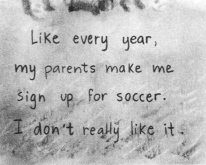

Like every year, my parents make me sign up for soccer. I don't really like it.

I'm not good at it.

The uniforms are too tight.

The other girls are cool.

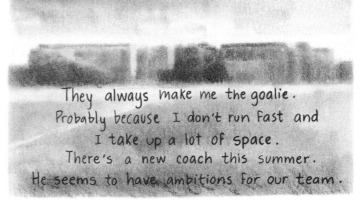

They always make me the goalie. Probably because I don't run fast and I take up a lot of space. There's a new coach this summer. He seems to have ambitions for our team.

You're going to be doing lots of running this summer, girls.

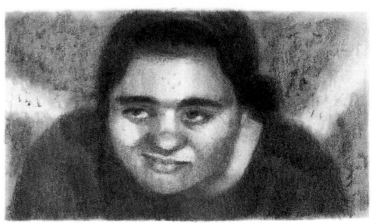

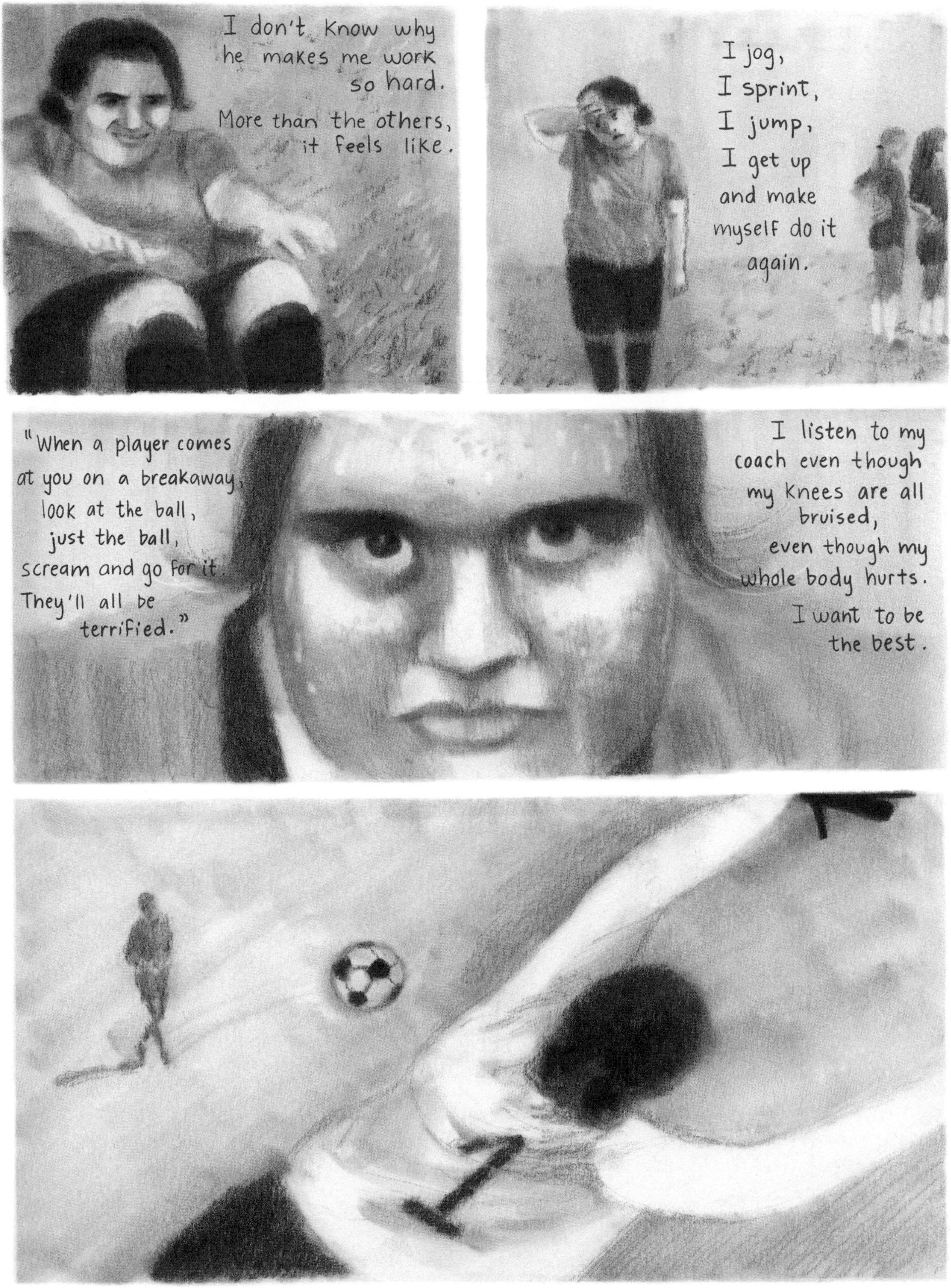
I don't know why he makes me work so hard.
More than the others, it feels like.
I jog, I sprint, I jump, I get up and make myself do it again.
"When a player comes at you on a breakaway, look at the ball, just the ball, scream and go for it. They'll all be terrified."
I listen to my coach even though my knees are all bruised, even though my whole body hurts.
I want to be the best.

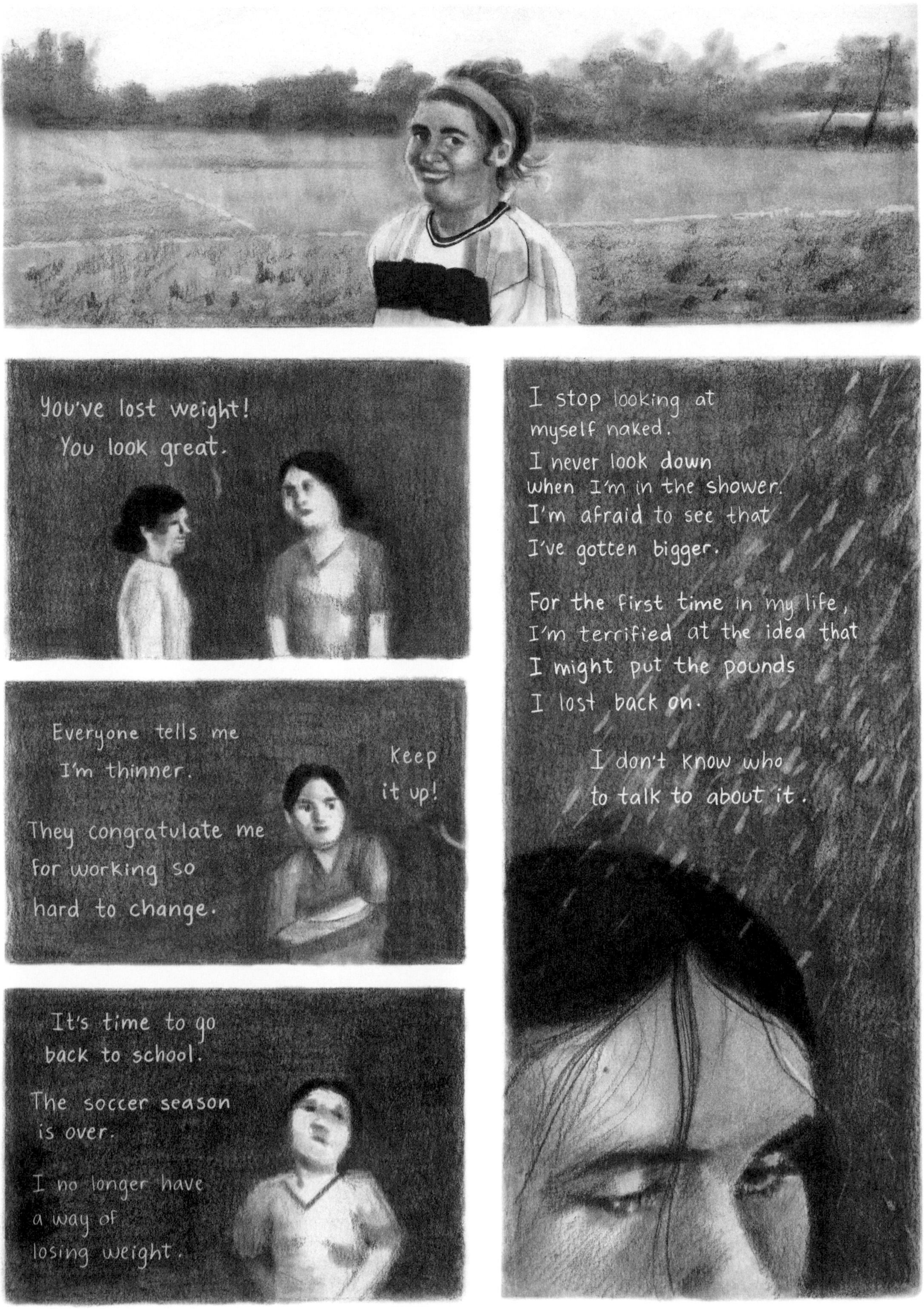
You've lost weight!
You look great.
Everyone tells me
I'm thinner.
Keep it up!
They congratulate me
for working so
hard to change.
It's time to go
back to school.
The soccer season
is over.
I no longer have
a way of
losing weight.
I stop looking at
myself naked.
I never look down
when I'm in the shower.
I'm afraid to see that
I've gotten bigger.
For the first time in my life,
I'm terrified at the idea that
I might put the pounds
I lost back on.
I don't know who
to talk to about it.

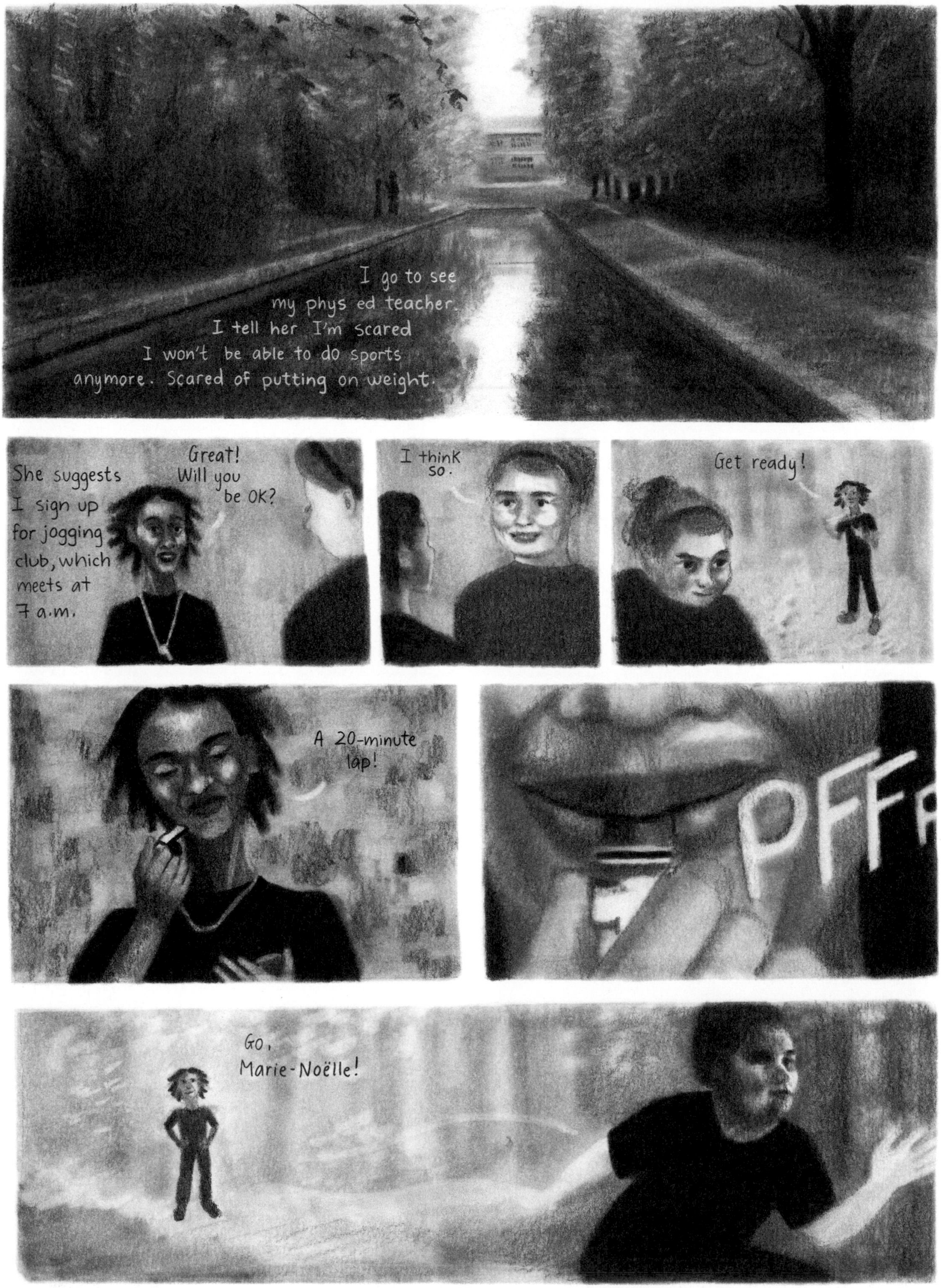
I go to see
my phys ed teacher.
I tell her I'm scared
I won't be able to do sports
anymore. Scared of putting on weight.
She suggests I sign up for jogging club, which meets at 7 a.m.
Great! Will you be OK?
I think so.
Get ready!
A 20-minute lap!
PFF
Go, Marie-Noëlle!

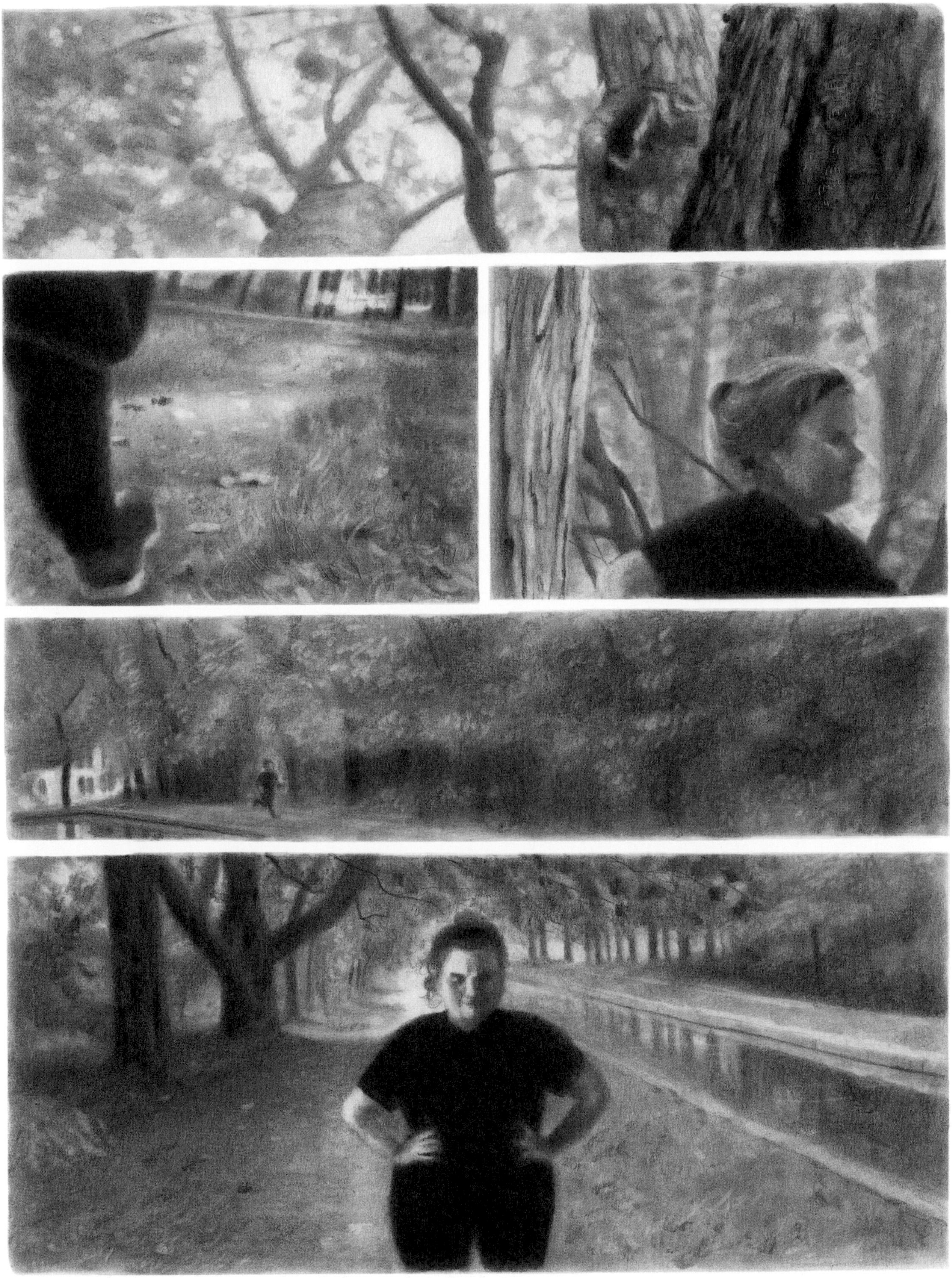

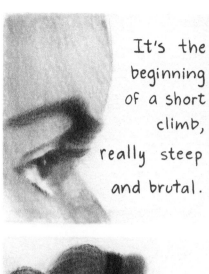

It's the beginning of a short climb, really steep and brutal.

A chance to lose weight fast.

A chance to have a body other than my own.

GO!

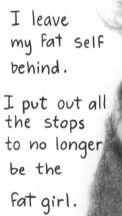

I leave my fat self behind.

I put out all the stops to no longer be the fat girl.

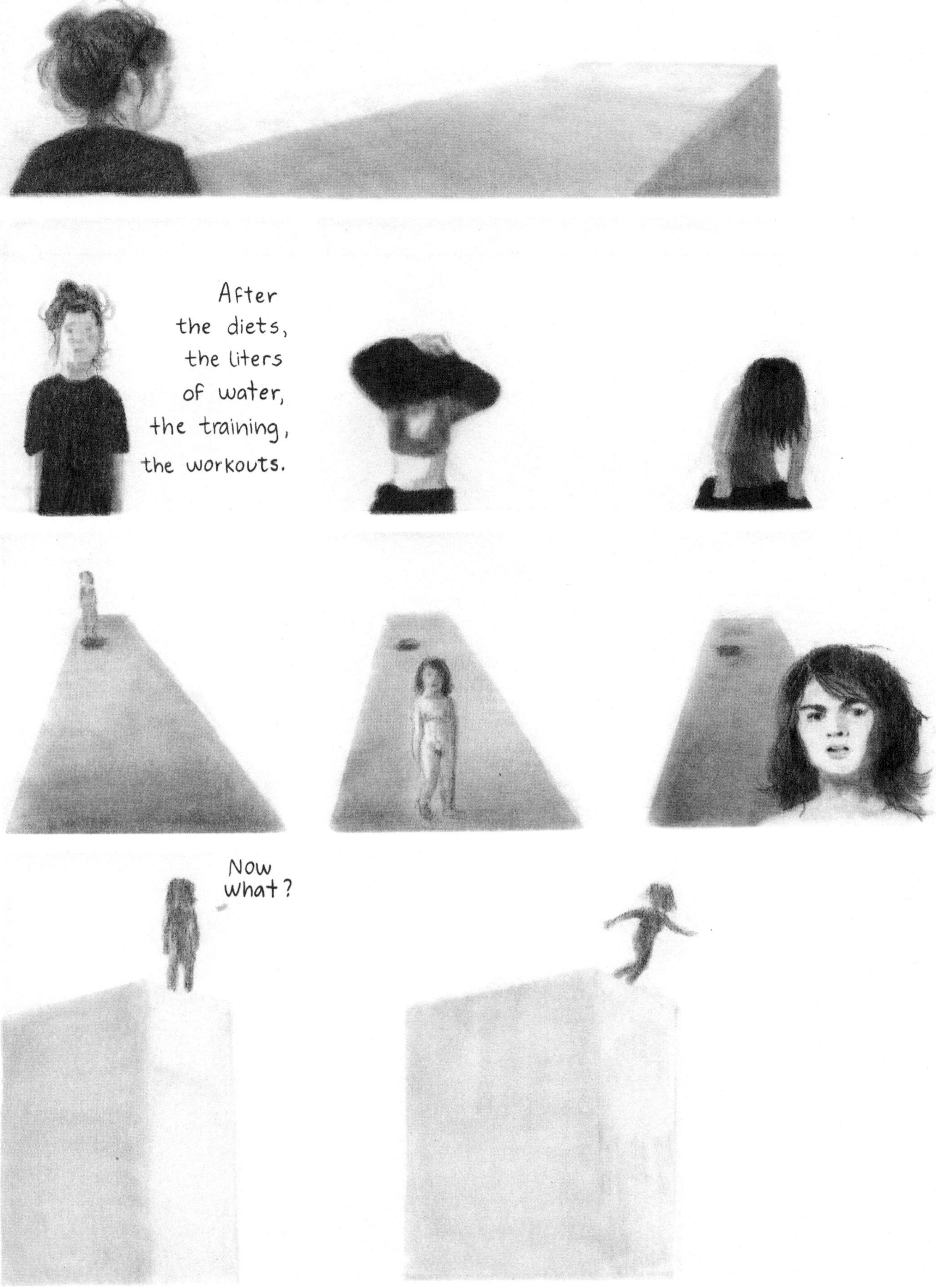
After
the diets,
the liters
of water,
the training,
the workouts.
Now
what?

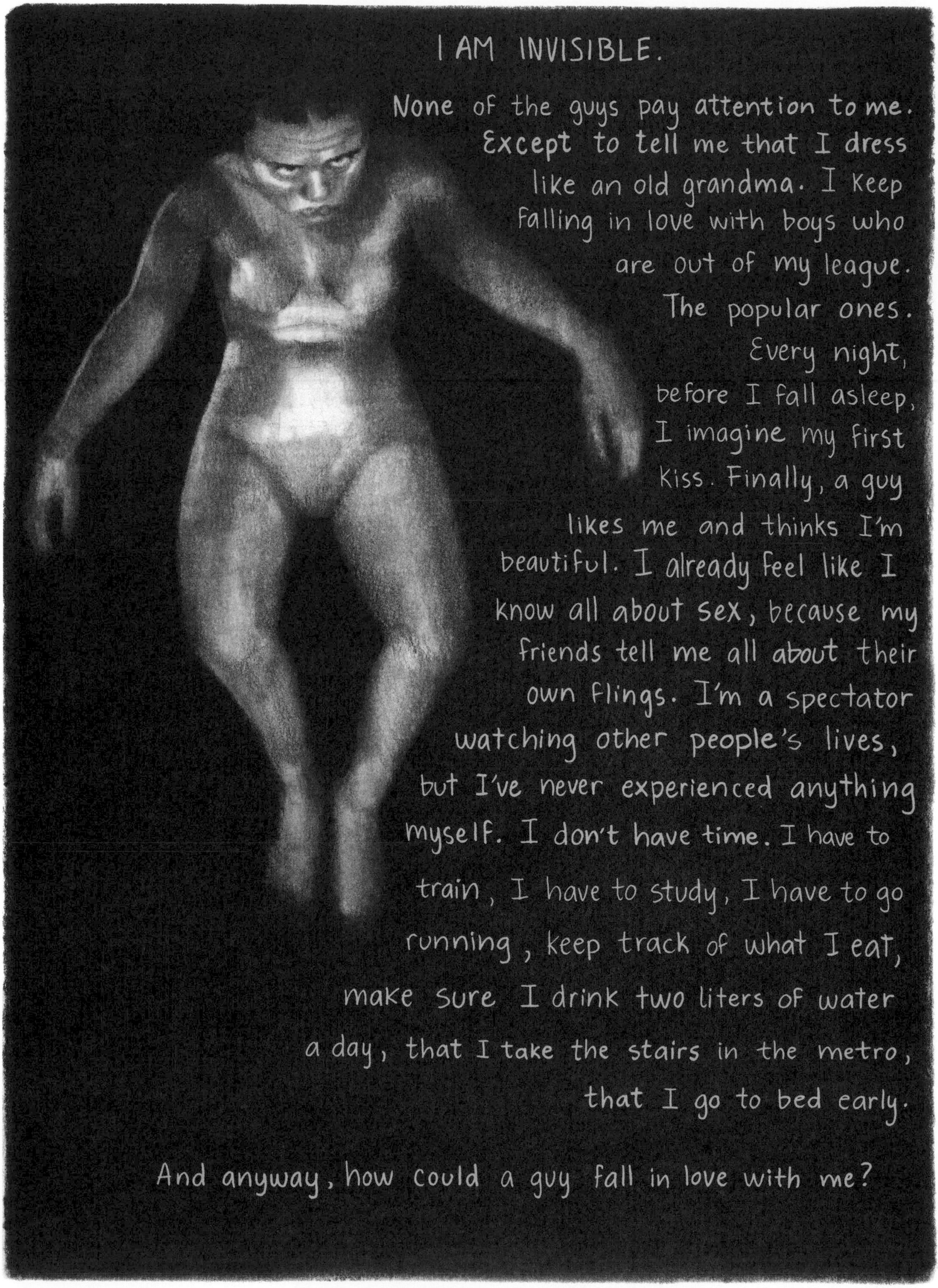
I AM INVISIBLE.
None of the guys pay attention to me. Except to tell me that I dress like an old grandma. I keep falling in love with boys who are out of my league. The popular ones. Every night, before I fall asleep, I imagine my first kiss. Finally, a guy likes me and thinks I'm beautiful. I already feel like I know all about sex, because my friends tell me all about their own flings. I'm a spectator watching other people's lives, but I've never experienced anything myself. I don't have time. I have to train, I have to study, I have to go running, keep track of what I eat, make sure I drink two liters of water a day, that I take the stairs in the metro, that I go to bed early.
And anyway, how could a guy fall in love with me?

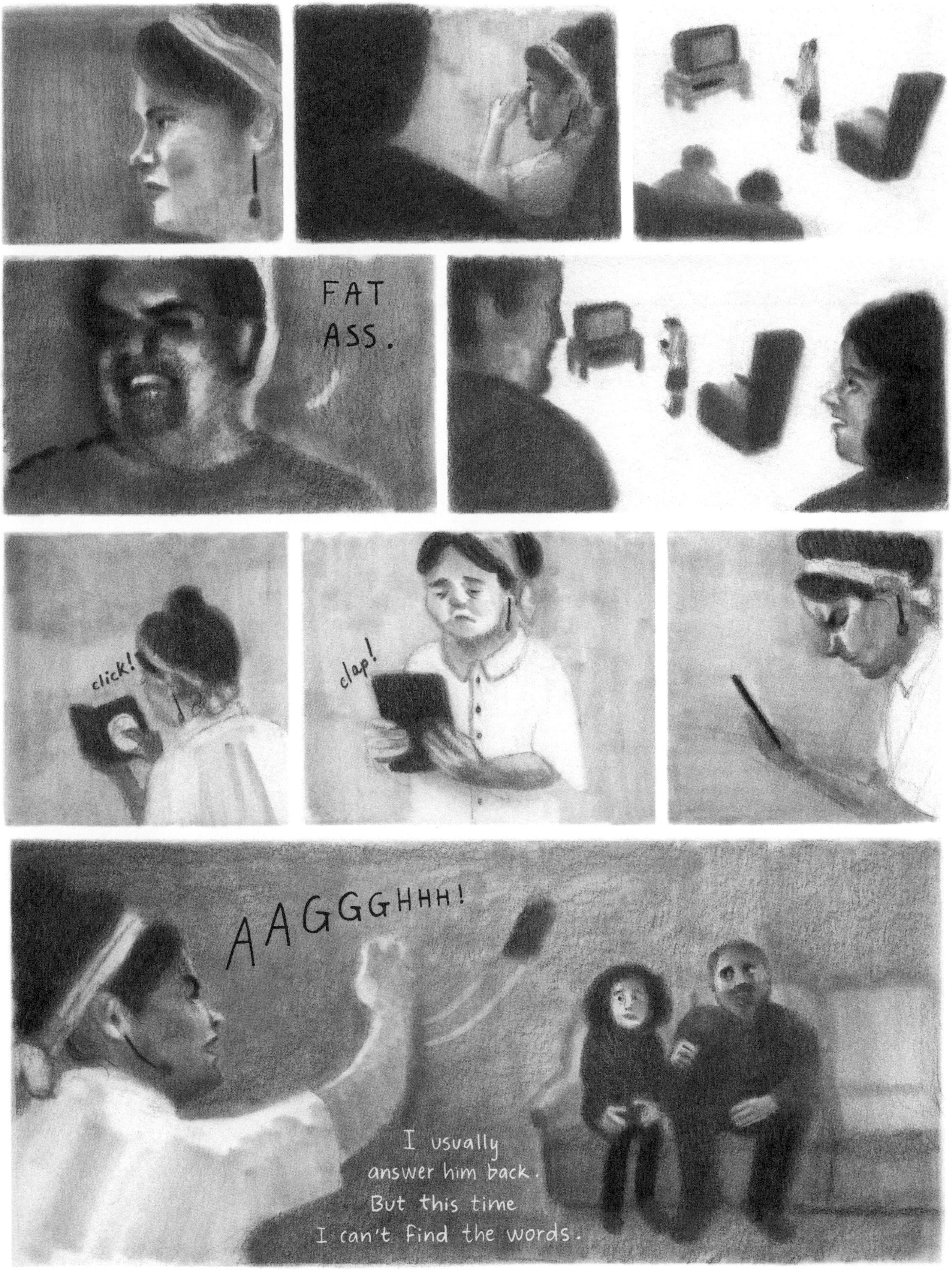
FAT ASS.
click!
clap!
AAGGGHHH!
I usually answer him back. But this time I can't find the words.

I leave.

17 years old.

I'm done with making an effort, with the sweat and pushing through.

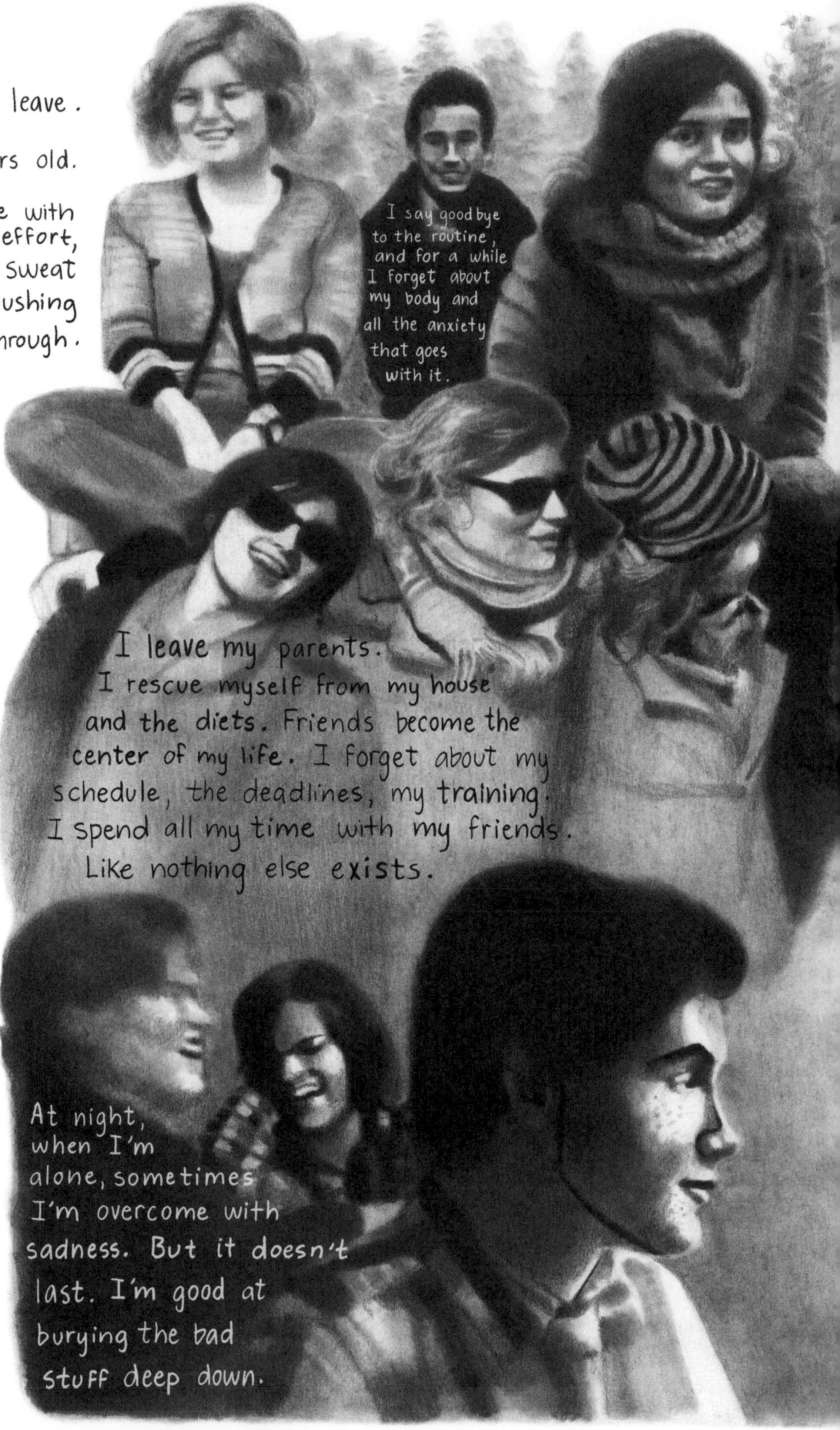
I say goodbye to the routine, and for a while I forget about my body and all the anxiety that goes with it.
I leave my parents. I rescue myself from my house and the diets. Friends become the center of my life. I forget about my schedule, the deadlines, my training. I spend all my time with my friends. Like nothing else exists.
At night, when I'm alone, sometimes I'm overcome with sadness. But it doesn't last. I'm good at burying the bad stuff deep down.

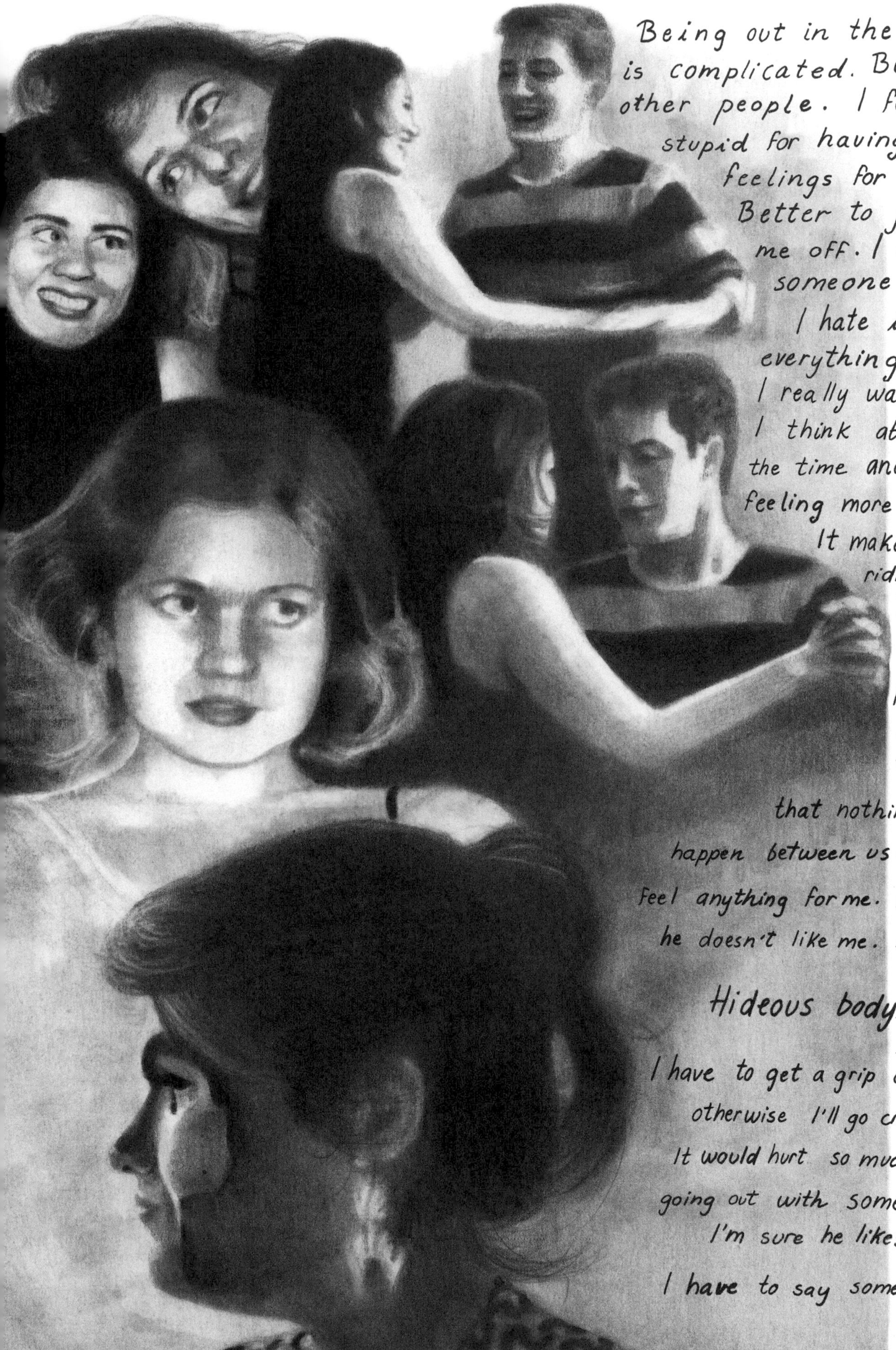

Being out in the world is complicated. Being around other people. I feel so stupid for having all these feelings for no reason. Better to just finish me off. I want to be someone else so much. I hate it. I hate everything. Me me me. I really want to die. I think about this guy all the time and it leaves me feeling more alone than ever. It makes me even more ridiculous. The ugly fat girl. I suddenly get it through my thick skull that nothing is going to happen between us. He doesn't feel anything for me. I'm so afraid he doesn't like me. It hurts.

Hideous body.

I have to get a grip on all of this, otherwise I'll go crazy. It would hurt so much to see him going out with someone else. I'm sure he likes me. I have to say something.

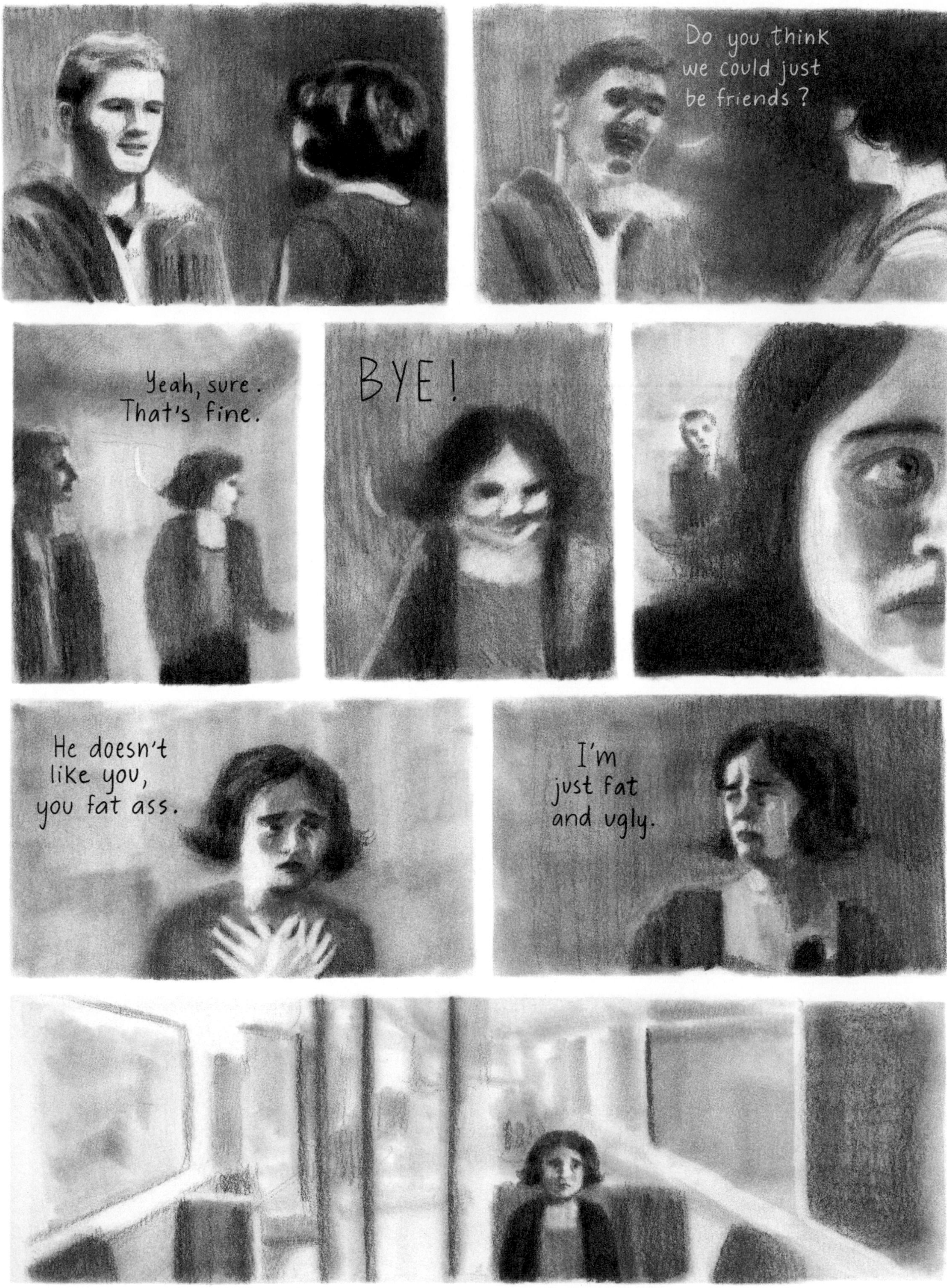
Do you think we could just be friends ?
Yeah, sure. That's fine.
BYE!
He doesn't like you, you fat ass.
I'm just fat and ugly.

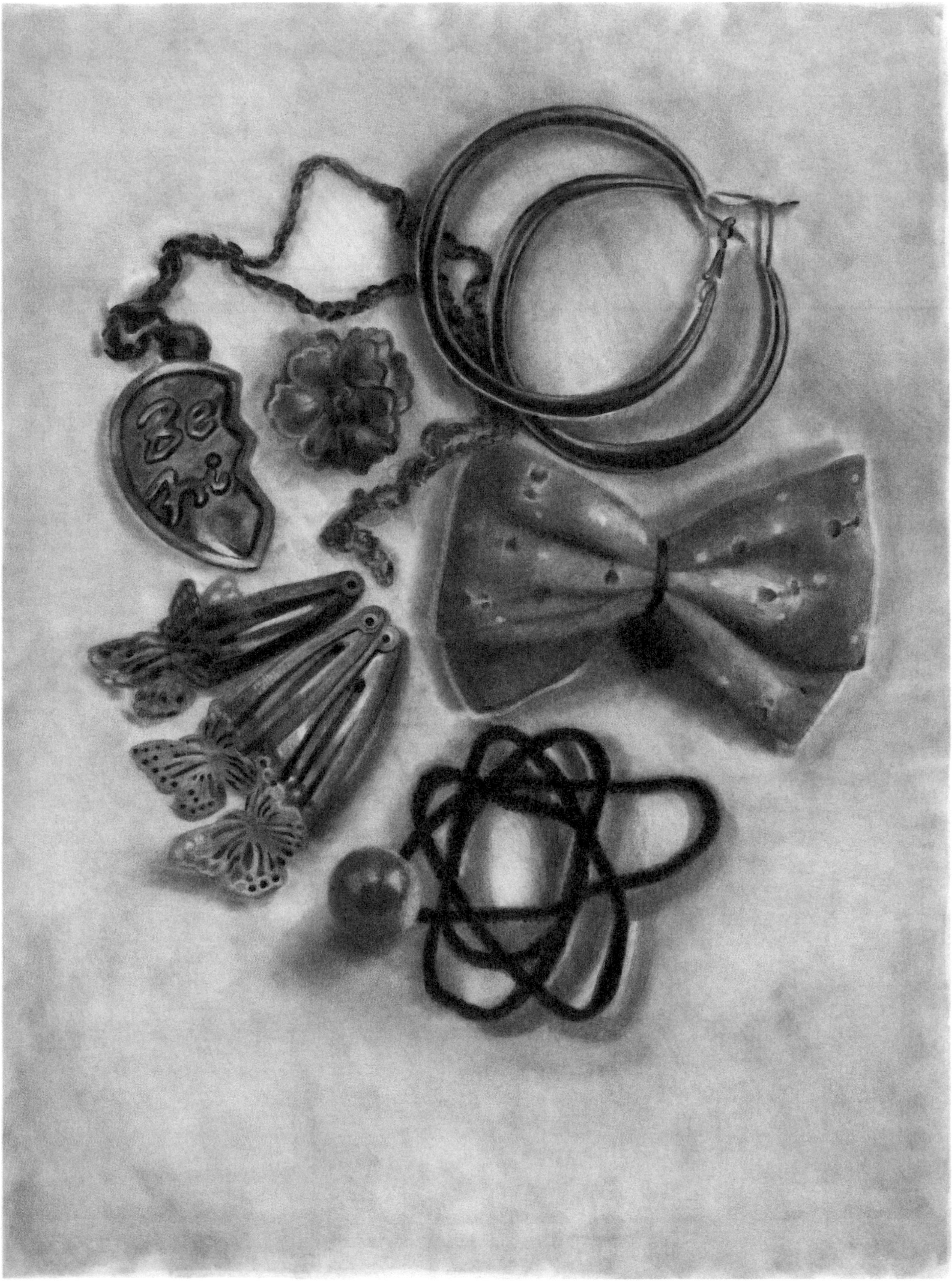
Be

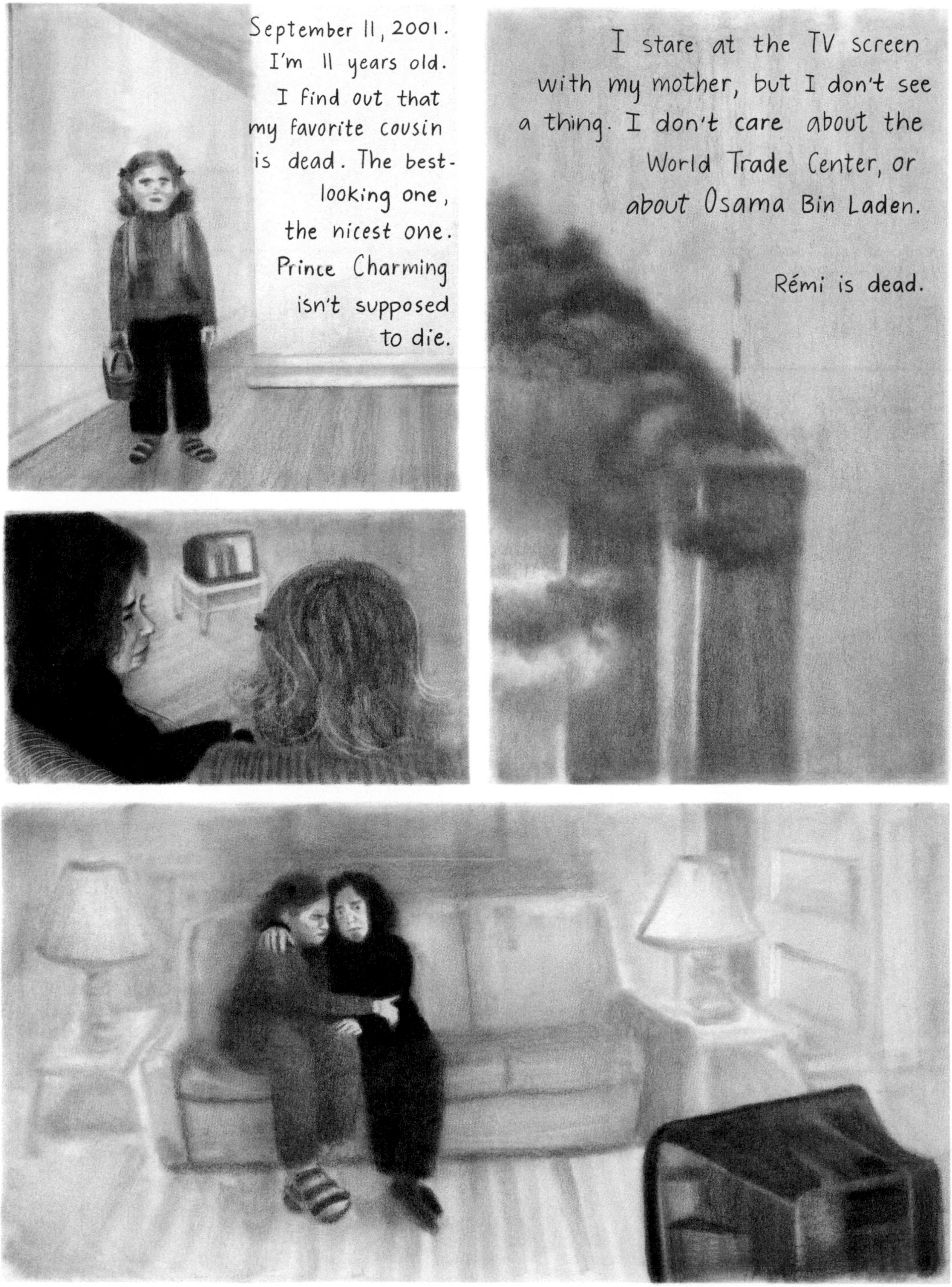
September 11, 2001. I'm 11 years old. I find out that my favorite cousin is dead. The best-looking one, the nicest one. Prince Charming isn't supposed to die.
I stare at the TV screen with my mother, but I don't see a thing. I don't care about the World Trade Center, or about Osama Bin Laden.
Rémi is dead.

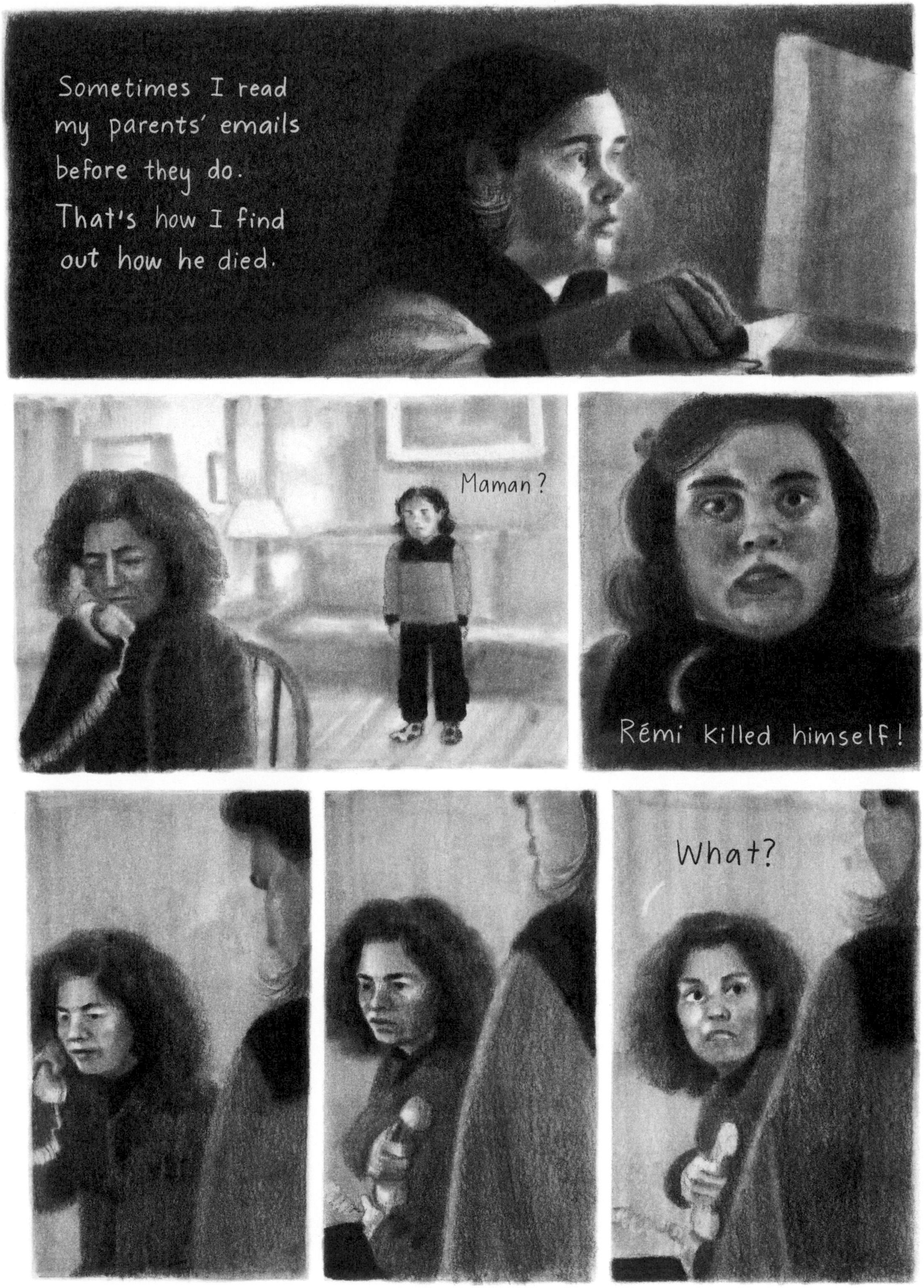
Sometimes I read my parents' emails before they do. That's how I find out how he died.
Maman?
Rémi killed himself!
What?

Before I go to sleep, I imagine going
back in time just to save Rémi.
I tell him not to jump.
And the violent act is wiped out and
everything goes back
to the way it was.

There is no more suicide.

Rémi.

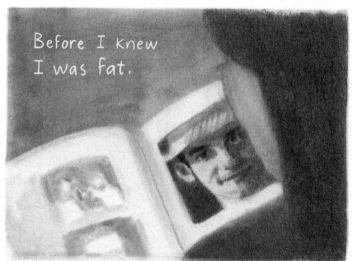

Before I knew
I was fat.

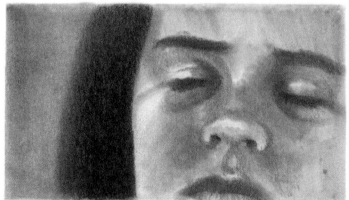

Before I
became the
ugly fat girl.

AT THE COTTAGE

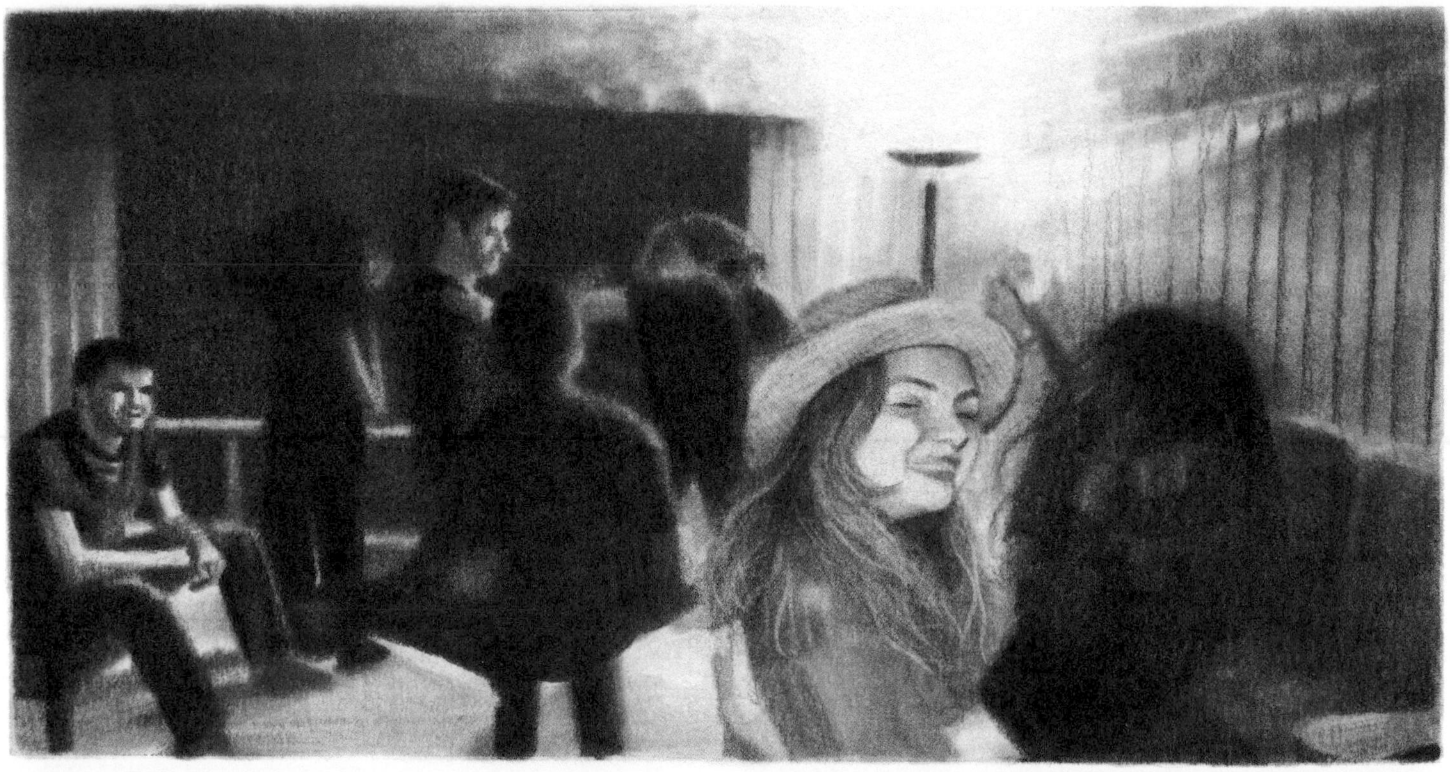

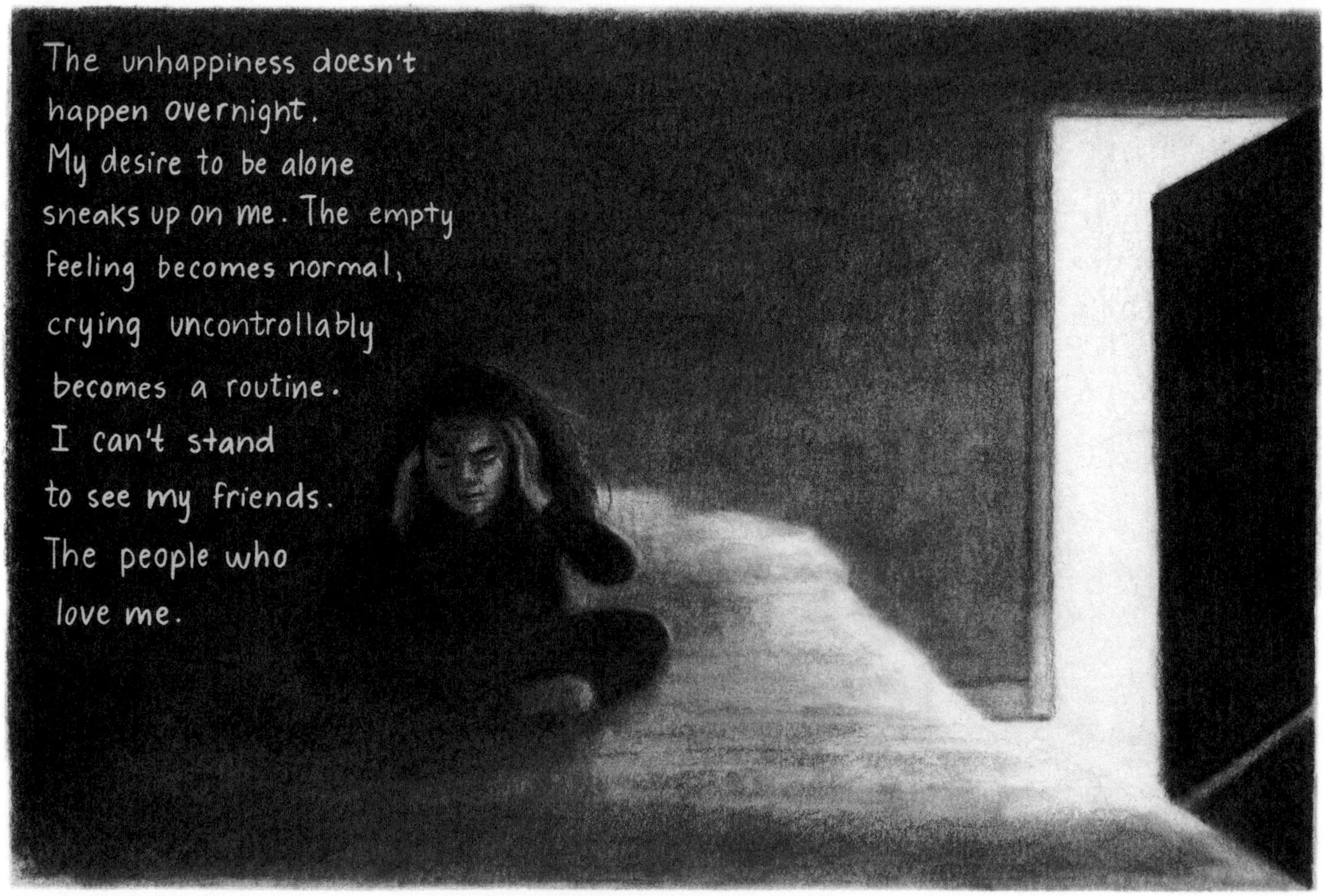
The unhappiness doesn't happen overnight. My desire to be alone sneaks up on me. The empty feeling becomes normal, crying uncontrollably becomes a routine. I can't stand to see my friends. The people who love me.

Then one day, I suddenly decide to break off with them. Dump them. Shut them out, too.

I find myself alone in my empty apartment.

Without them, I can dive into this sea of dark thoughts.

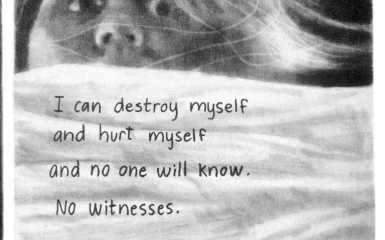

I can destroy myself and hurt myself and no one will know.

No witnesses.

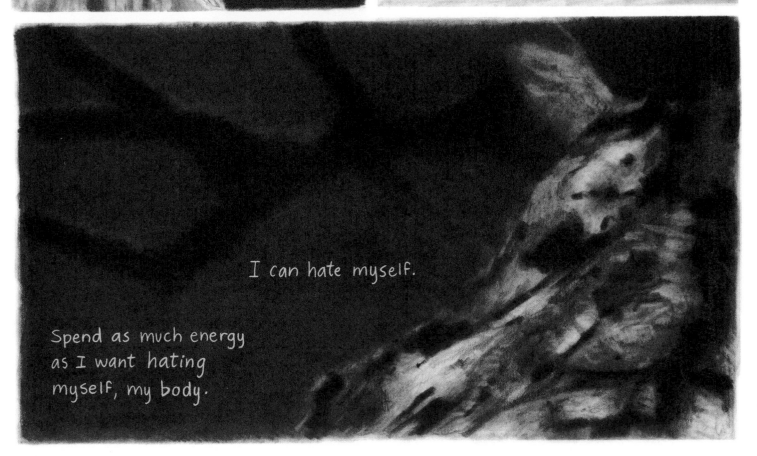

I can hate myself.

Spend as much energy as I want hating myself, my body.

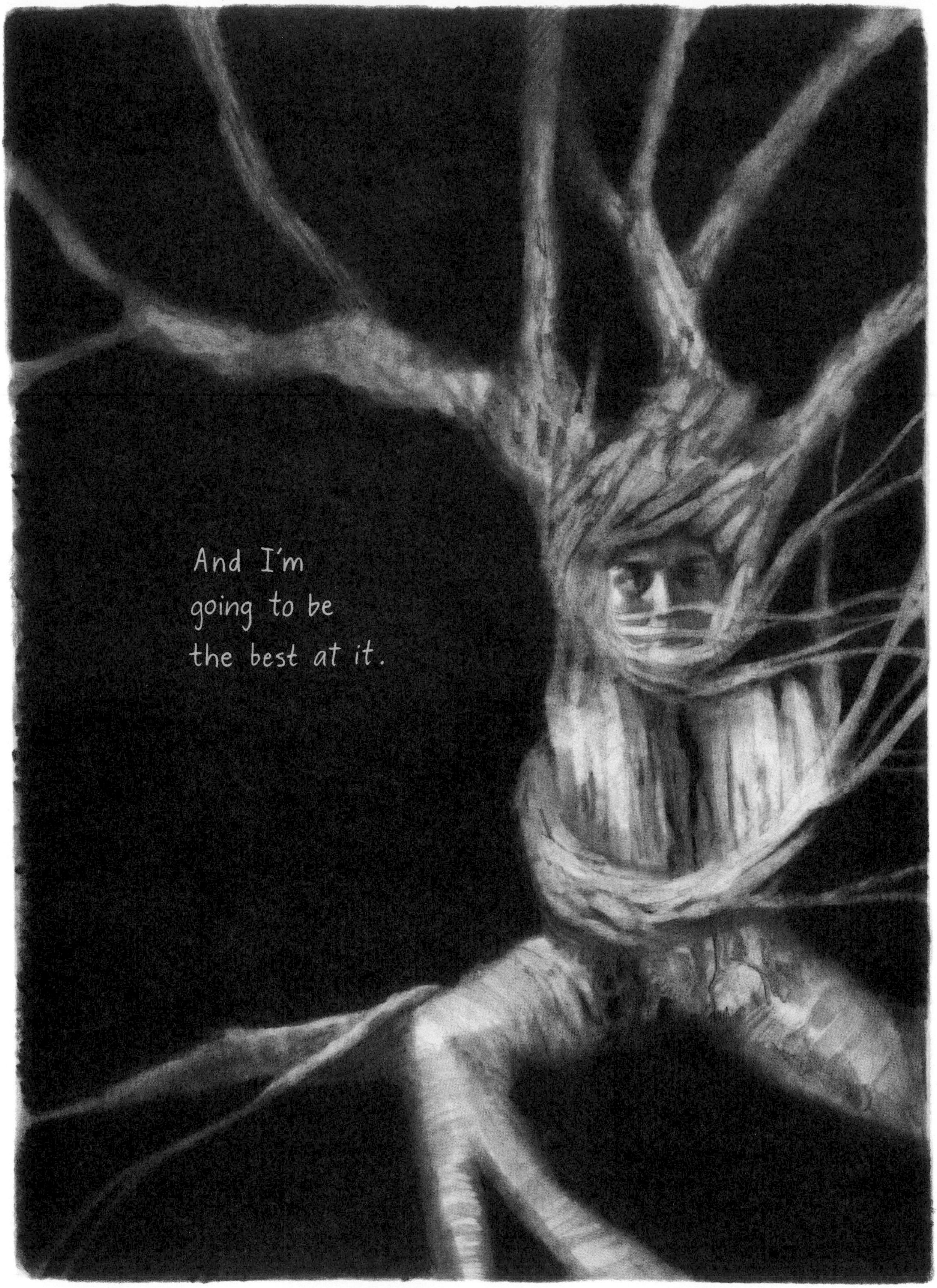
And I'm
going to be
the best at it.

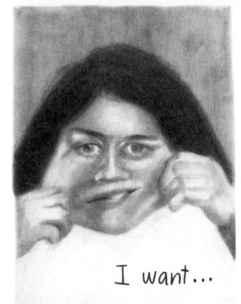 I want...

 ...to rip off...

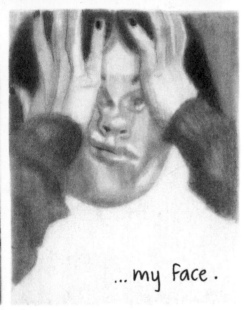 ...my face.

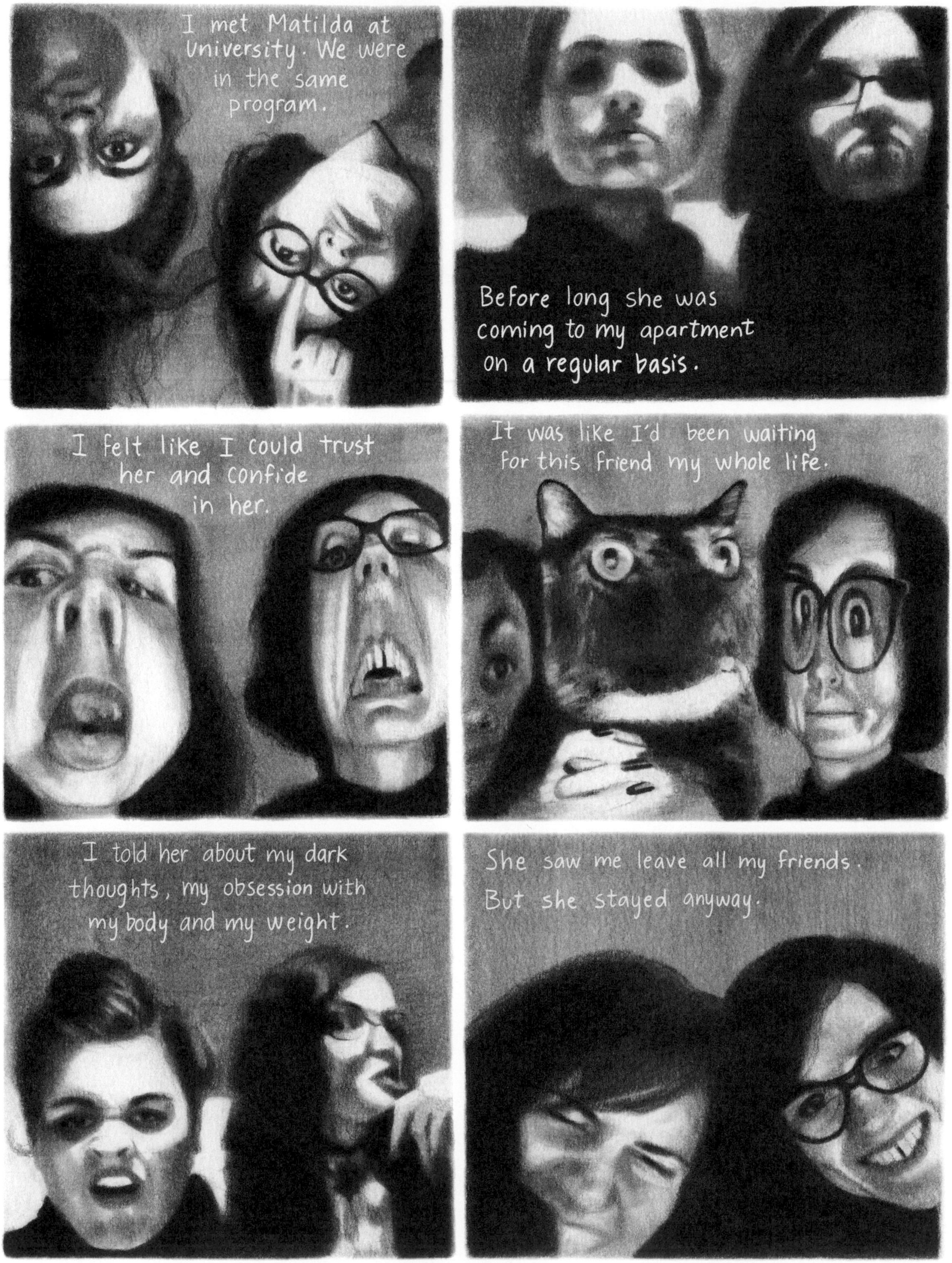
I met Matilda at University. We were in the same program.
Before long she was coming to my apartment on a regular basis.
I felt like I could trust her and confide in her.
It was like I'd been waiting for this friend my whole life.
I told her about my dark thoughts, my obsession with my body and my weight.
She saw me leave all my friends. But she stayed anyway.

I'm not happy.

I need someone.

Right now it's this

fucking pressure that hurts.

It's a pressure on my chest.

I want to cry,

to get free of this fucking body.

To get free of me.

I want to be in love.

I want someone to love me back.

I want it so much.

DEADLINE 23.

I can't take it anymore.

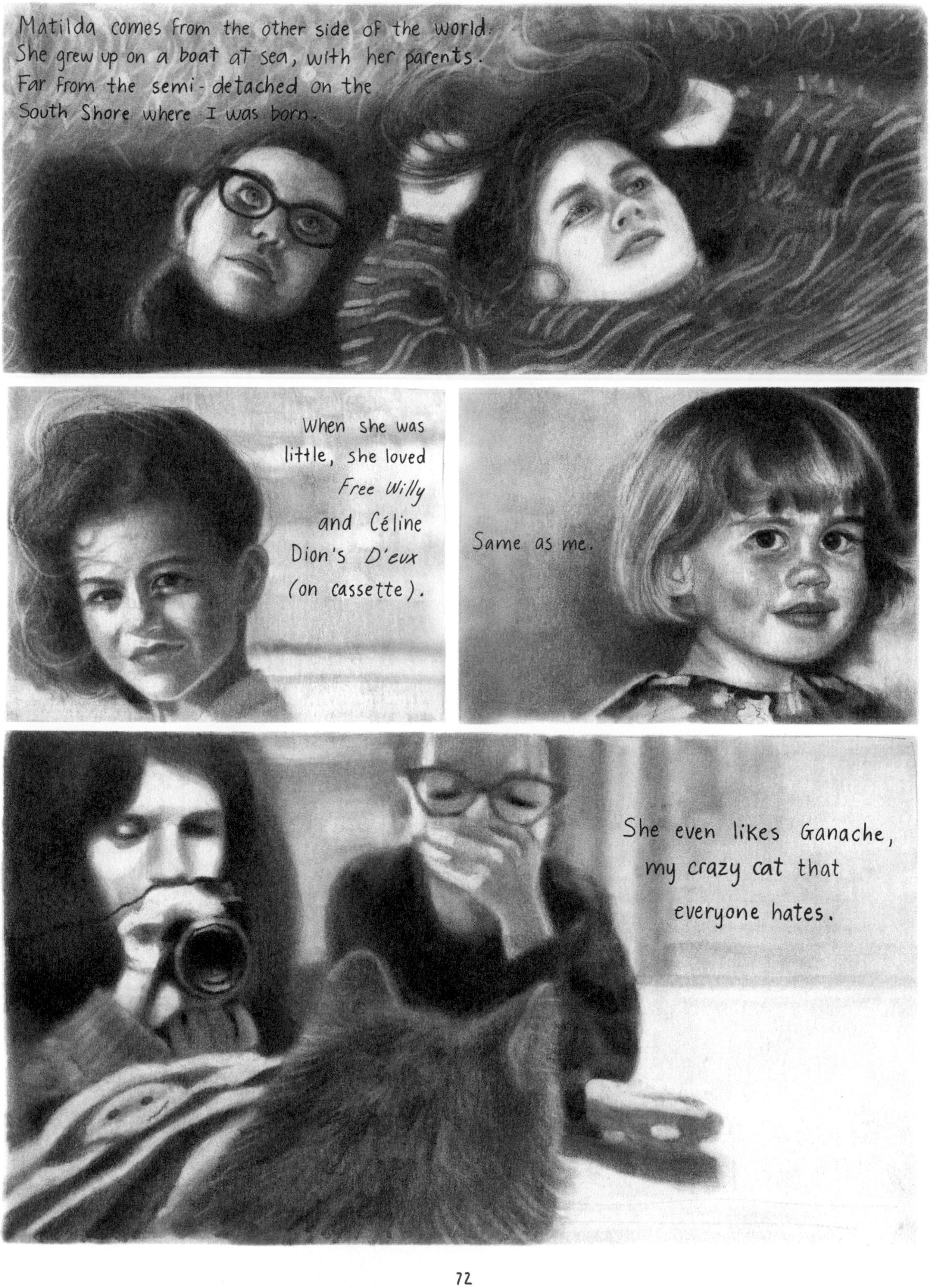
Matilda comes from the other side of the world. She grew up on a boat at sea, with her parents. Far from the semi-detached on the South Shore where I was born.
When she was little, she loved *Free Willy* and Céline Dion's *D'eux* (on cassette).
Same as me.
She even likes Ganache, my crazy cat that everyone hates.

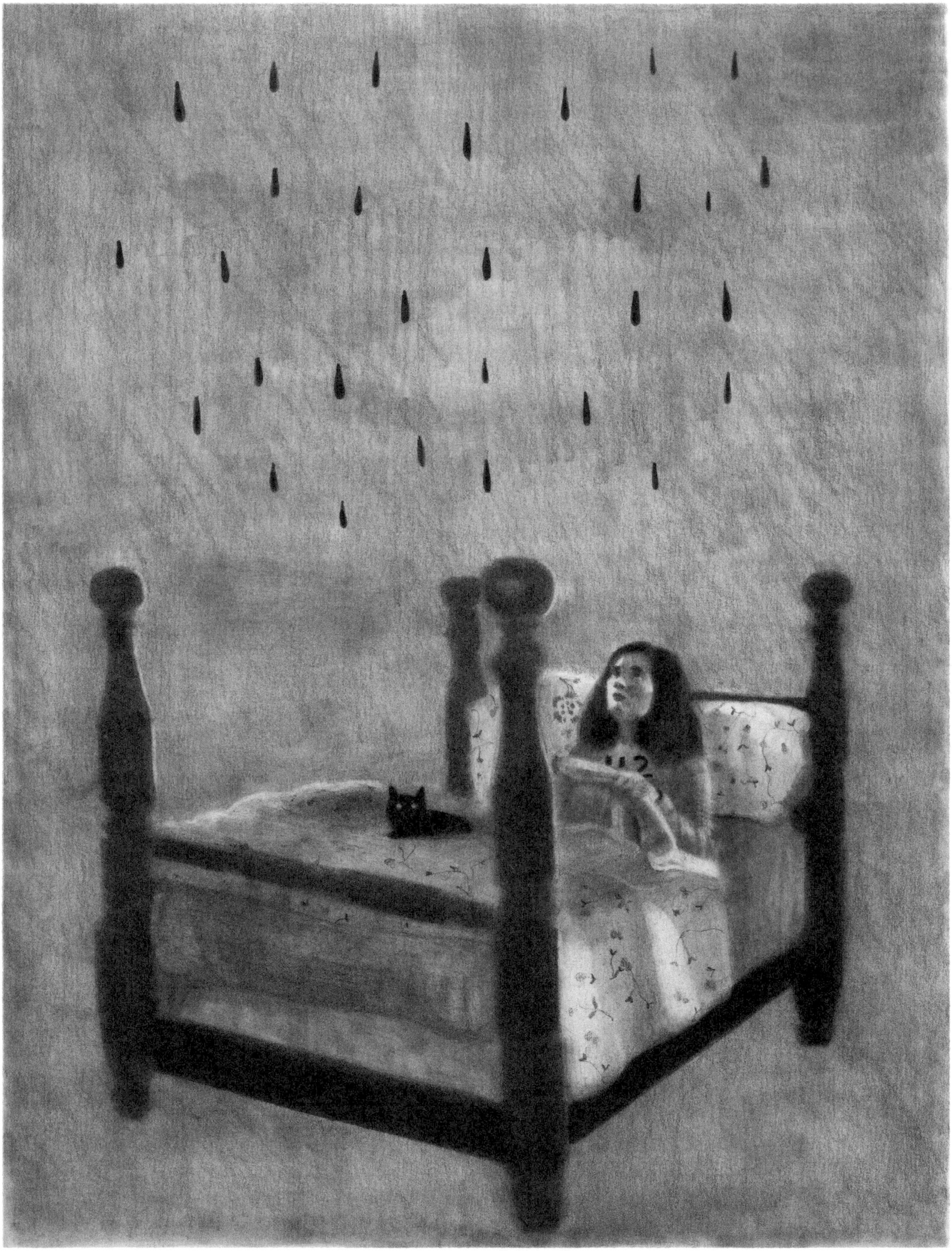

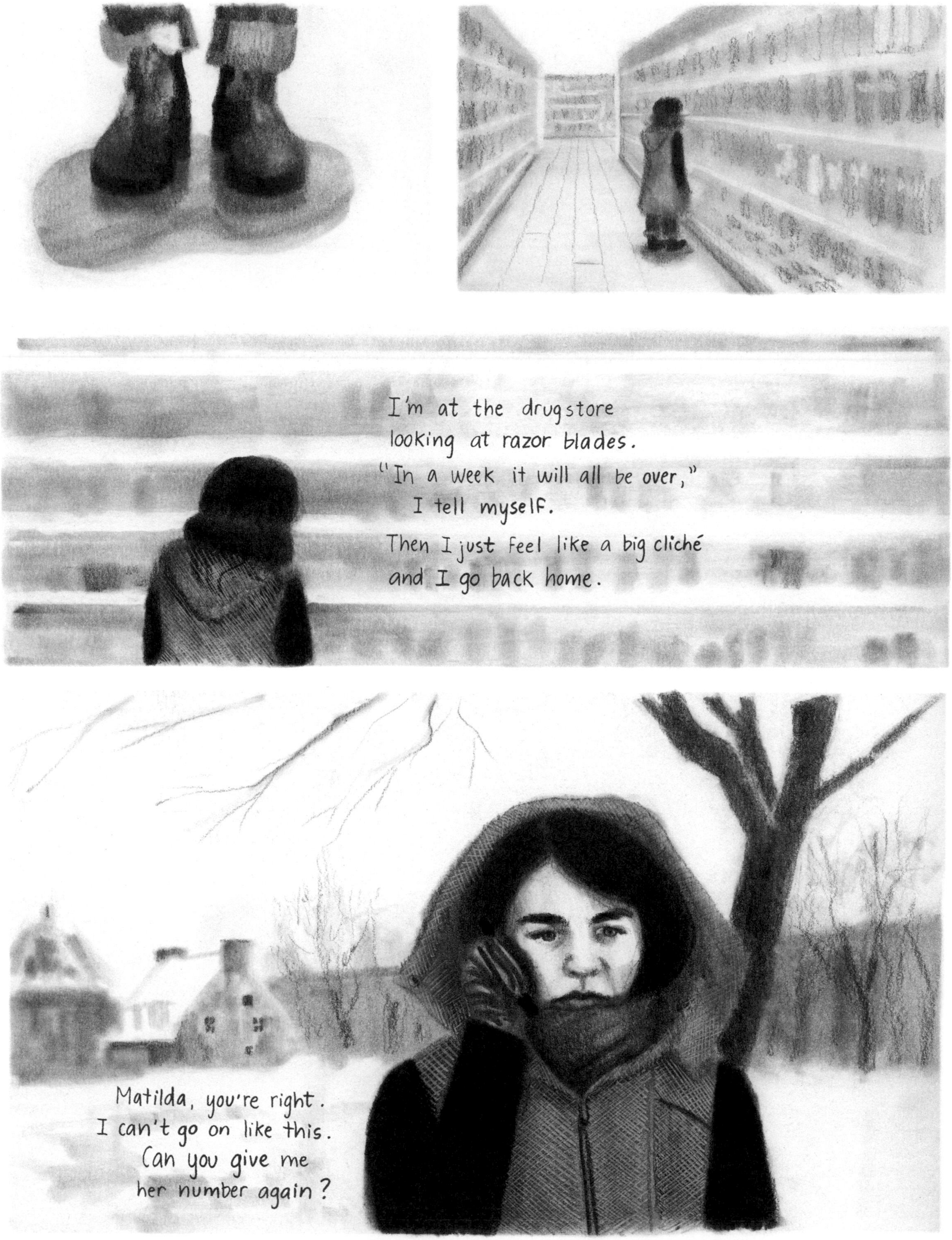
I'm at the drugstore
looking at razor blades.
"In a week it will all be over,"
I tell myself.
Then I just feel like a big cliché
and I go back home.
Matilda, you're right.
I can't go on like this.
Can you give me
her number again?

It is the first time anyone has suggested I go and talk to someone.

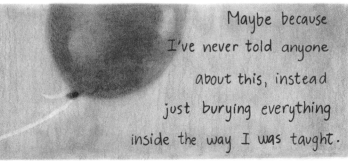
Maybe because I've never told anyone about this, instead just burying everything inside the way I was taught.

You'll wait for me?

Yes.
Don't worry.

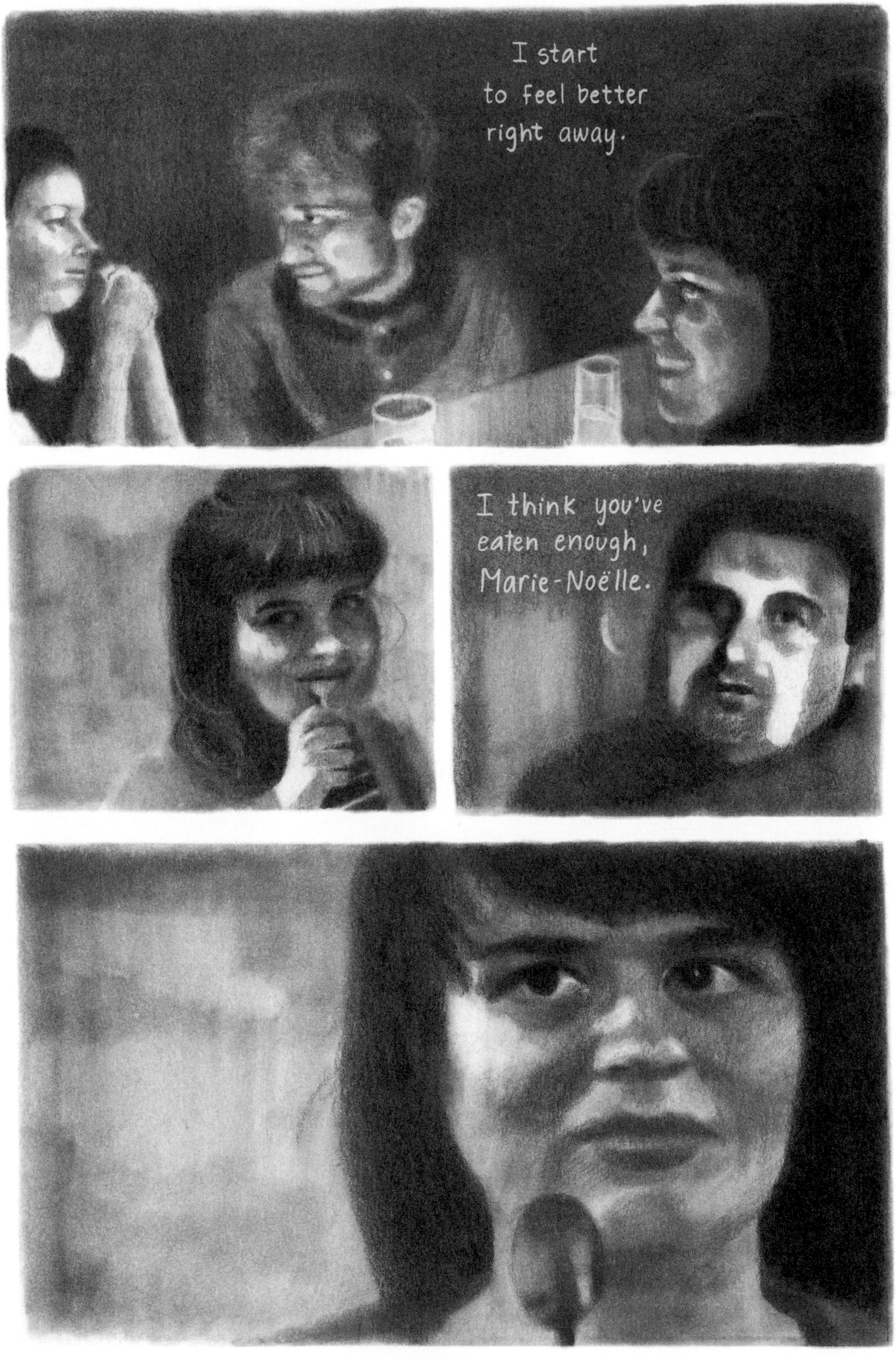
I start to feel better right away.
I think you've eaten enough, Marie-Noëlle.

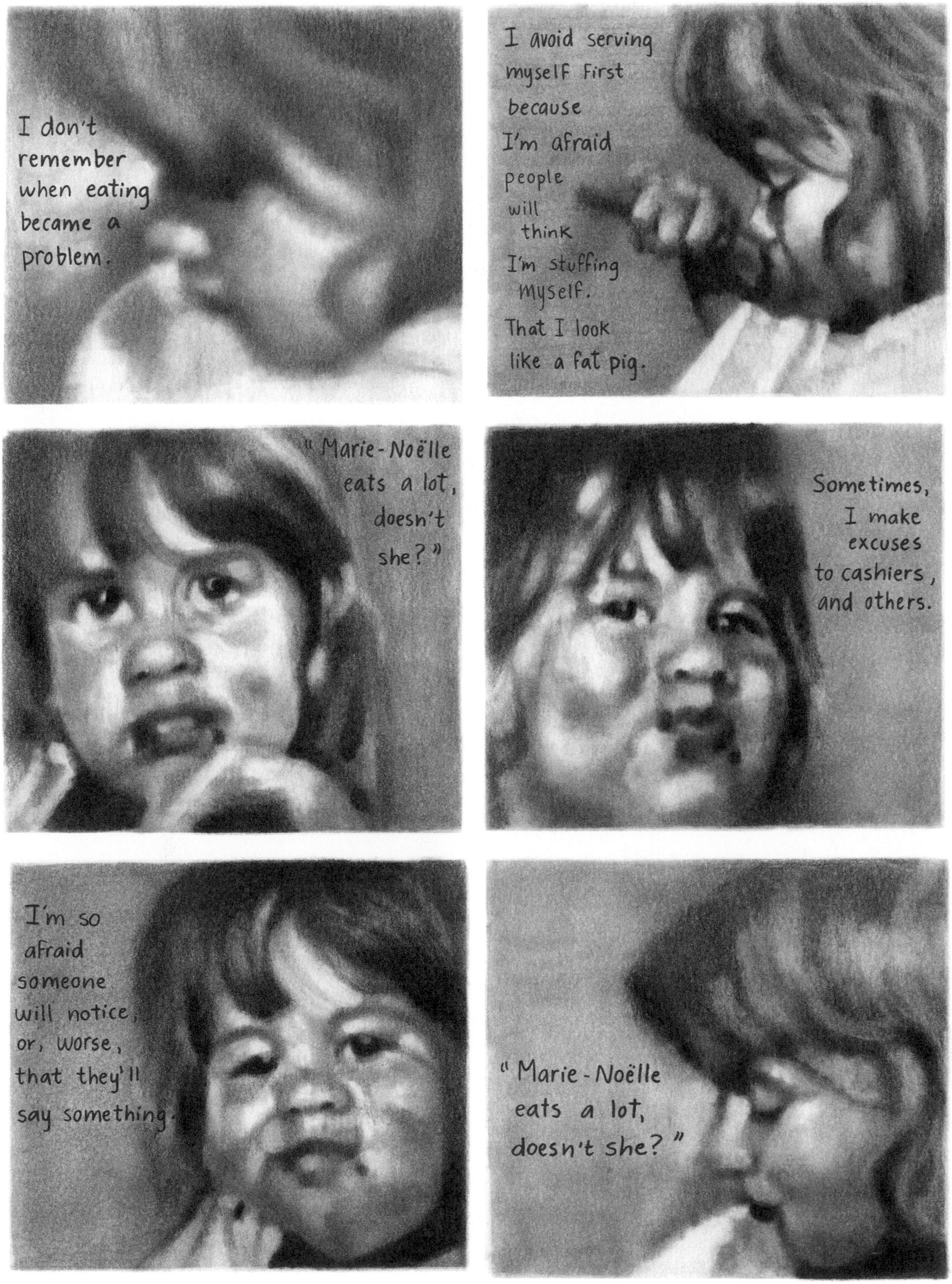
I don't remember when eating became a problem.
I avoid serving myself first because I'm afraid people will think I'm stuffing myself. That I look like a fat pig.
"Marie-Noëlle eats a lot, doesn't she?"
Sometimes, I make excuses to cashiers, and others.
I'm so afraid someone will notice, or, worse, that they'll say something.
"Marie-Noëlle eats a lot, doesn't she?"

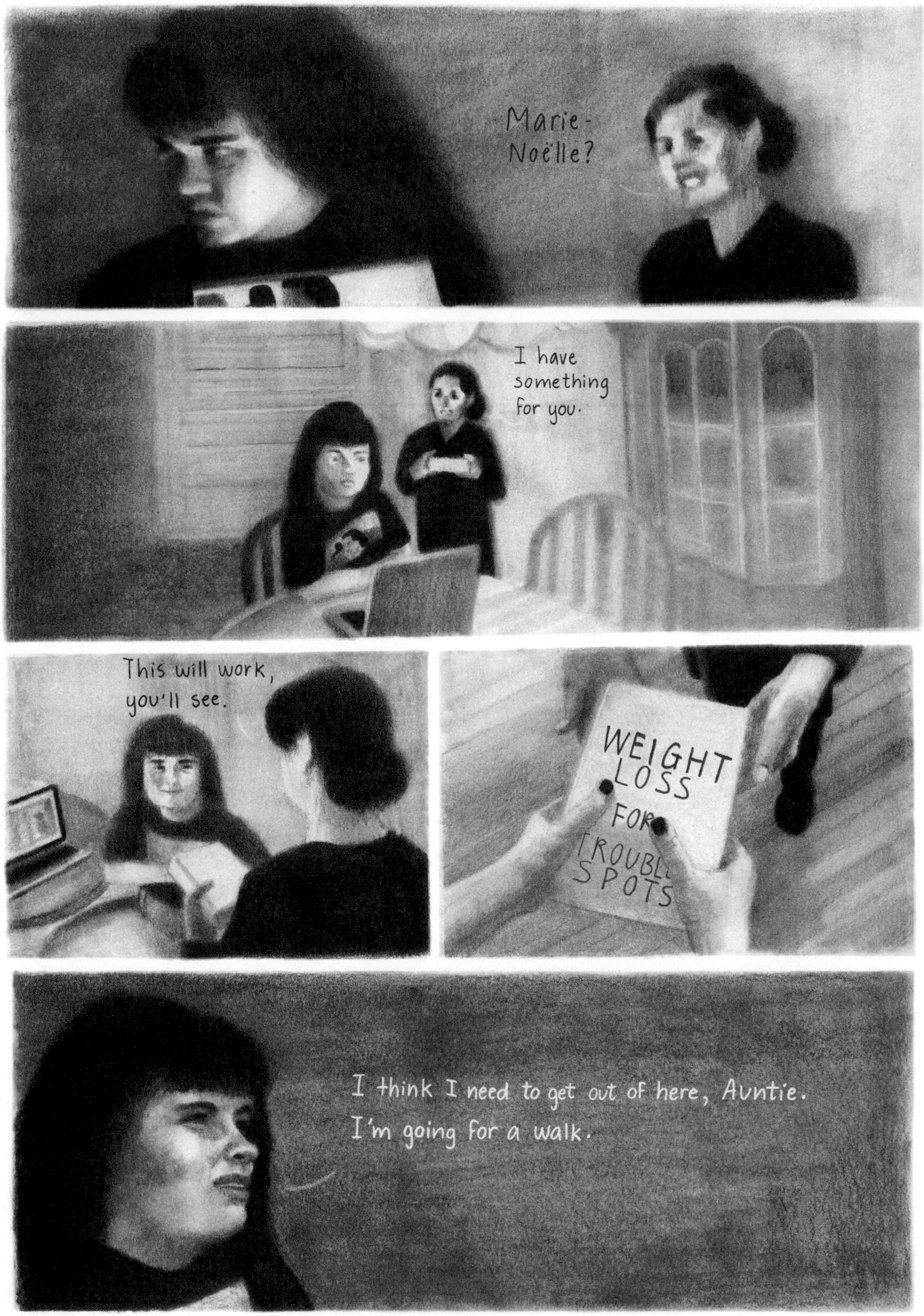
Marie-Noëlle?
I have something for you.
This will work, you'll see.
WEIGHT LOSS FOR TROUBLE SPOTS
I think I need to get out of here, Auntie. I'm going for a walk.

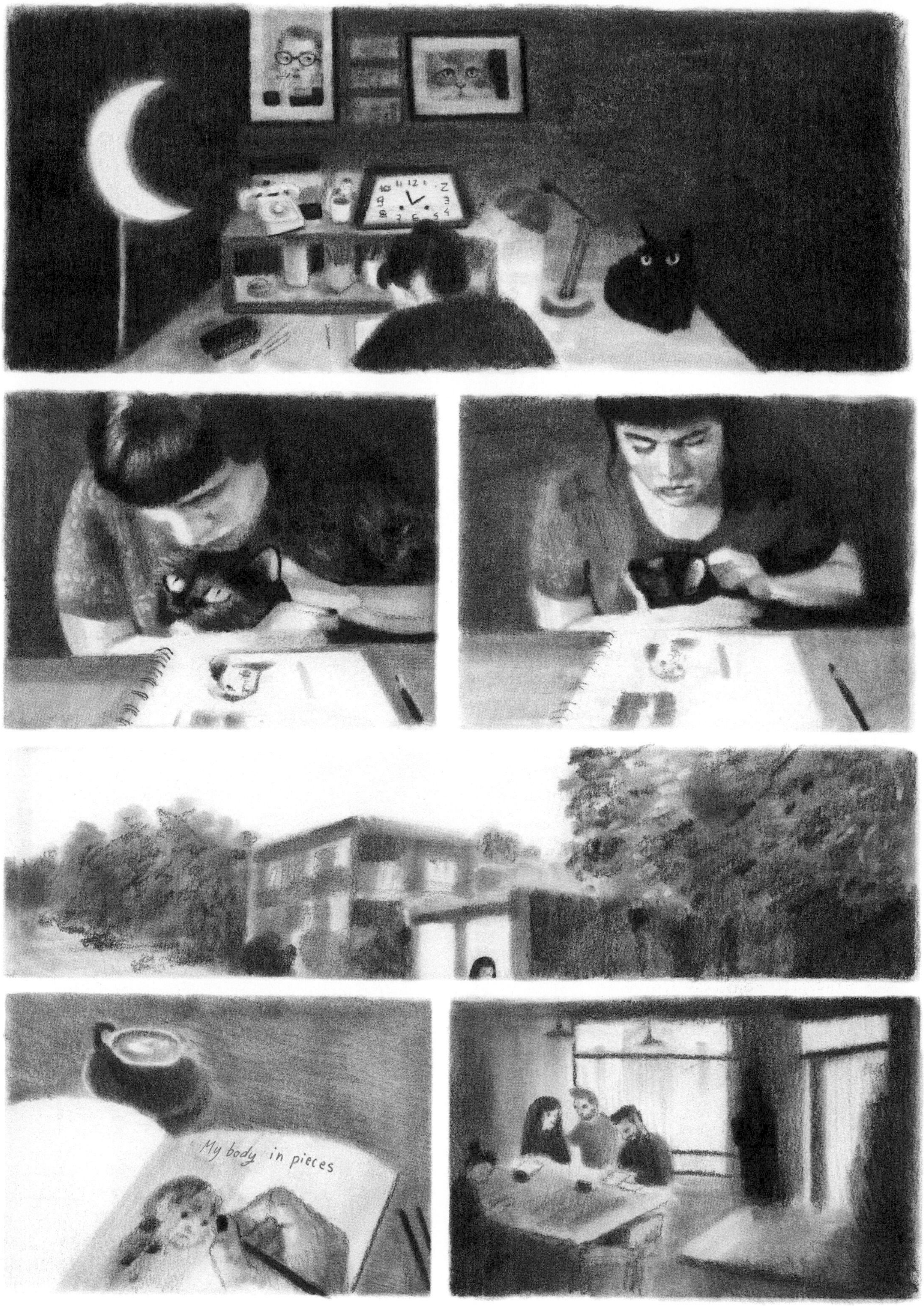
My body in pieces

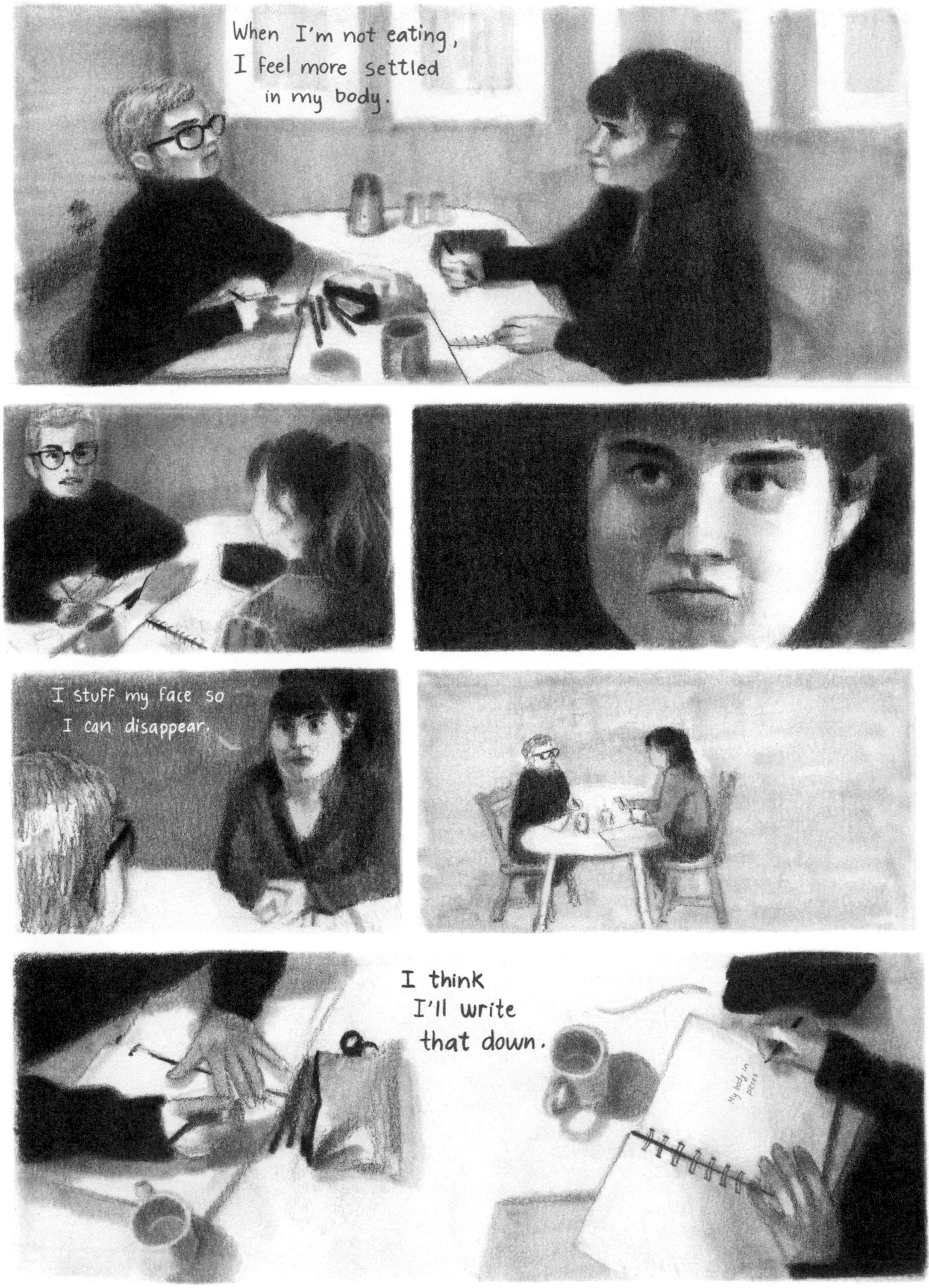
When I'm not eating, I feel more settled in my body.
I stuff my face so I can disappear.
I think I'll write that down.
My body in pieces

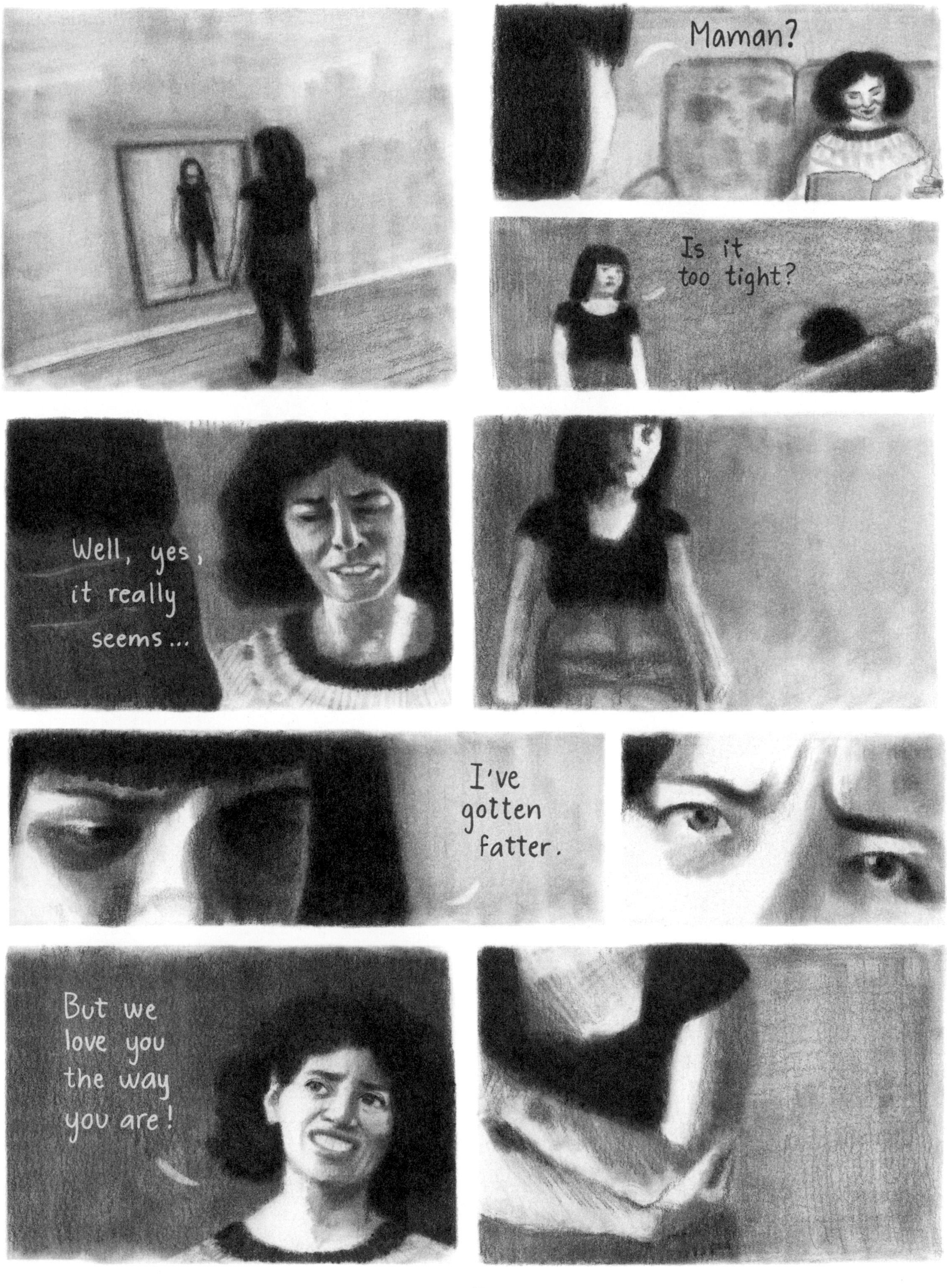
Maman?
Is it too tight?
Well, yes, it really seems...
I've gotten fatter.
But we love you the way you are!

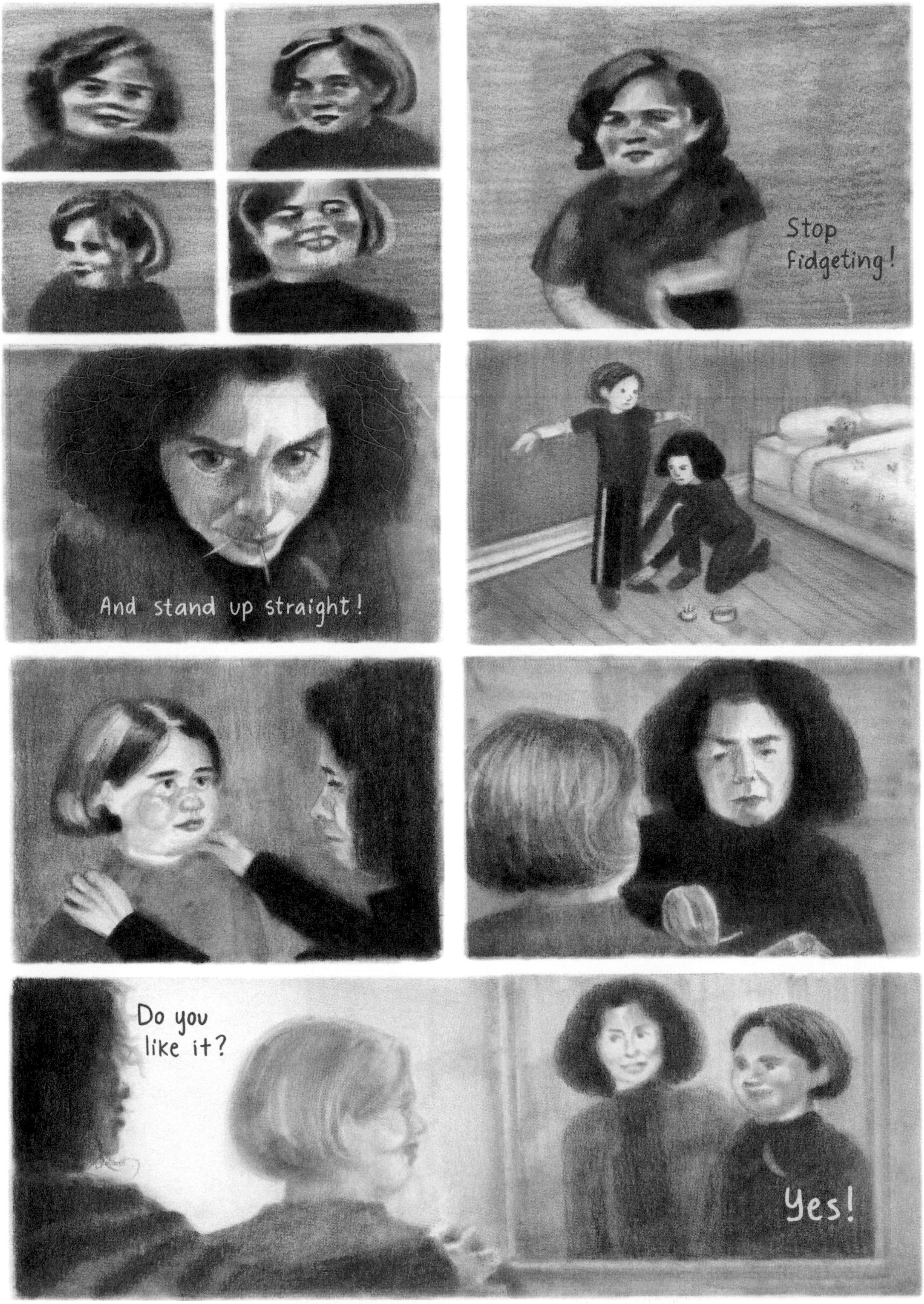

Stop fidgeting!
And stand up straight!
Do you like it?
Yes!

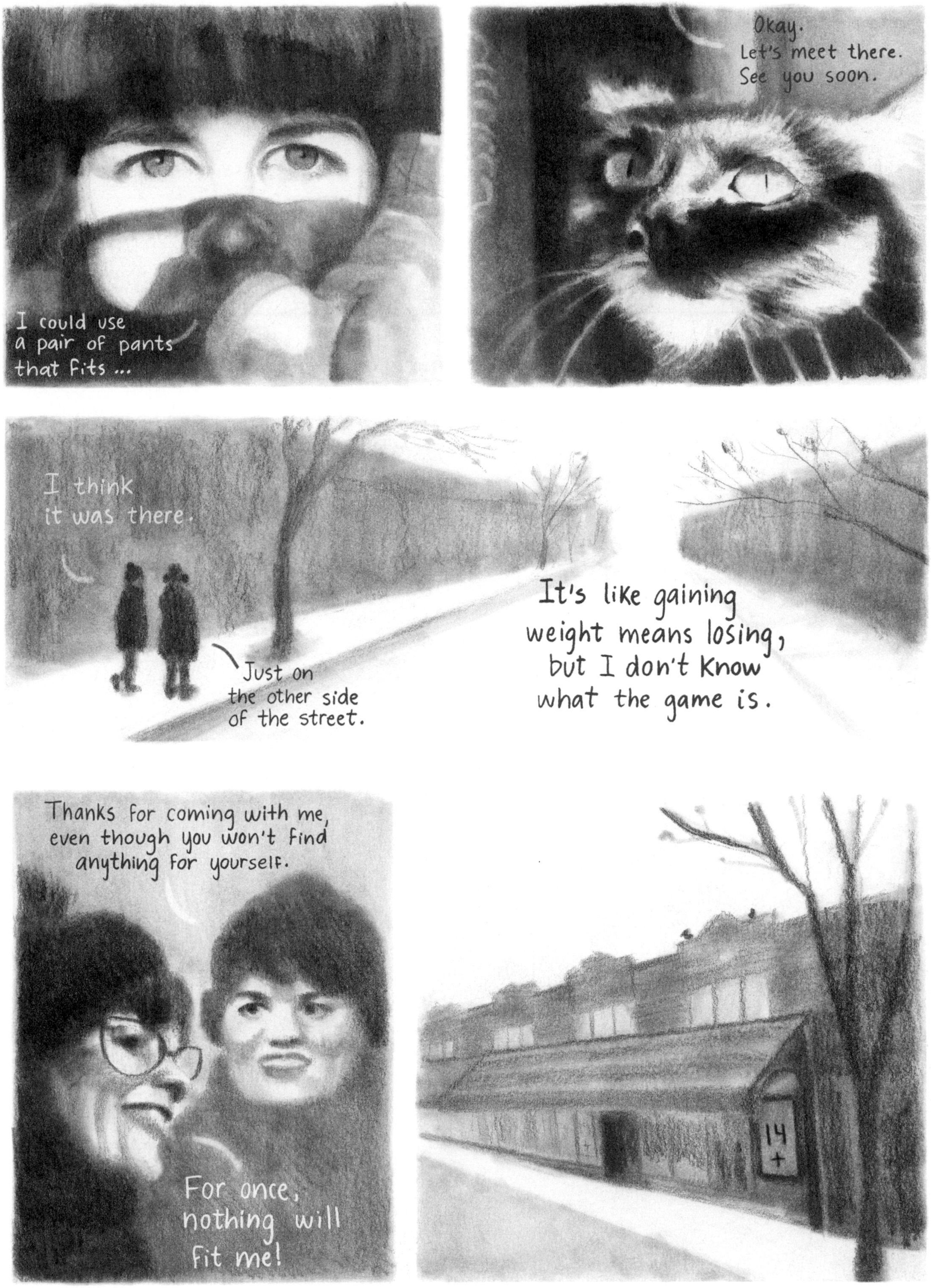
I could use a pair of pants that fits ...
Okay. Let's meet there. See you soon.
I think it was there.
Just on the other side of the street.
It's like gaining weight means losing, but I don't know what the game is.
Thanks for coming with me, even though you won't find anything for yourself.
For once, nothing will fit me!
14+

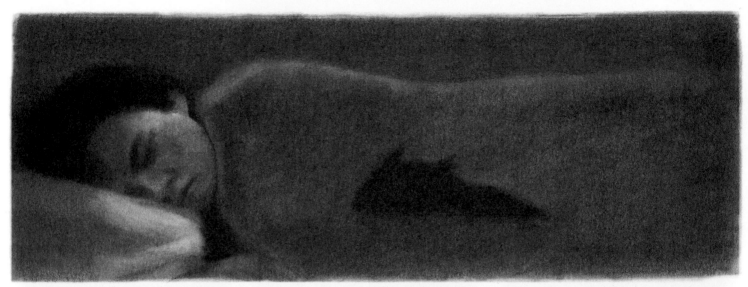

I haven't worked out in two weeks.

I have to pull myself together. I have to stop eating bread. No milk in my coffee.

I have to start doing sit-ups again before bed. Have to stop eating potatoes, too...

...I have to...

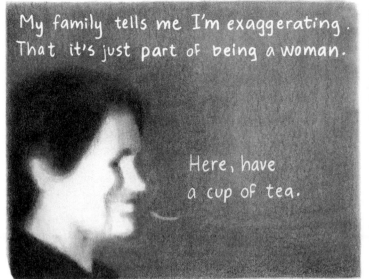

My family tells me I'm exaggerating. That it's just part of being a woman.

Here, have a cup of tea.

Women pass down their body shame from generation to generation.

Thank you, Auntie.

You'll see, you'll lose it all...

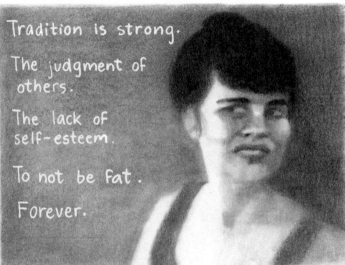

Tradition is strong.

The judgment of others.

The lack of self-esteem.

To not be fat.

Forever.

They thought it was more important to teach me how to hold in my stomach than teach me to stand up and be proud of myself.

Like that!

It's hard, a childhood full of Barbies and princesses that all look the same.

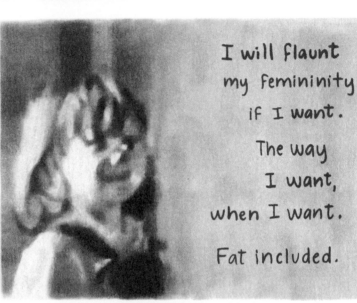

I will flaunt my femininity if I want.

The way I want, when I want.

Fat included.

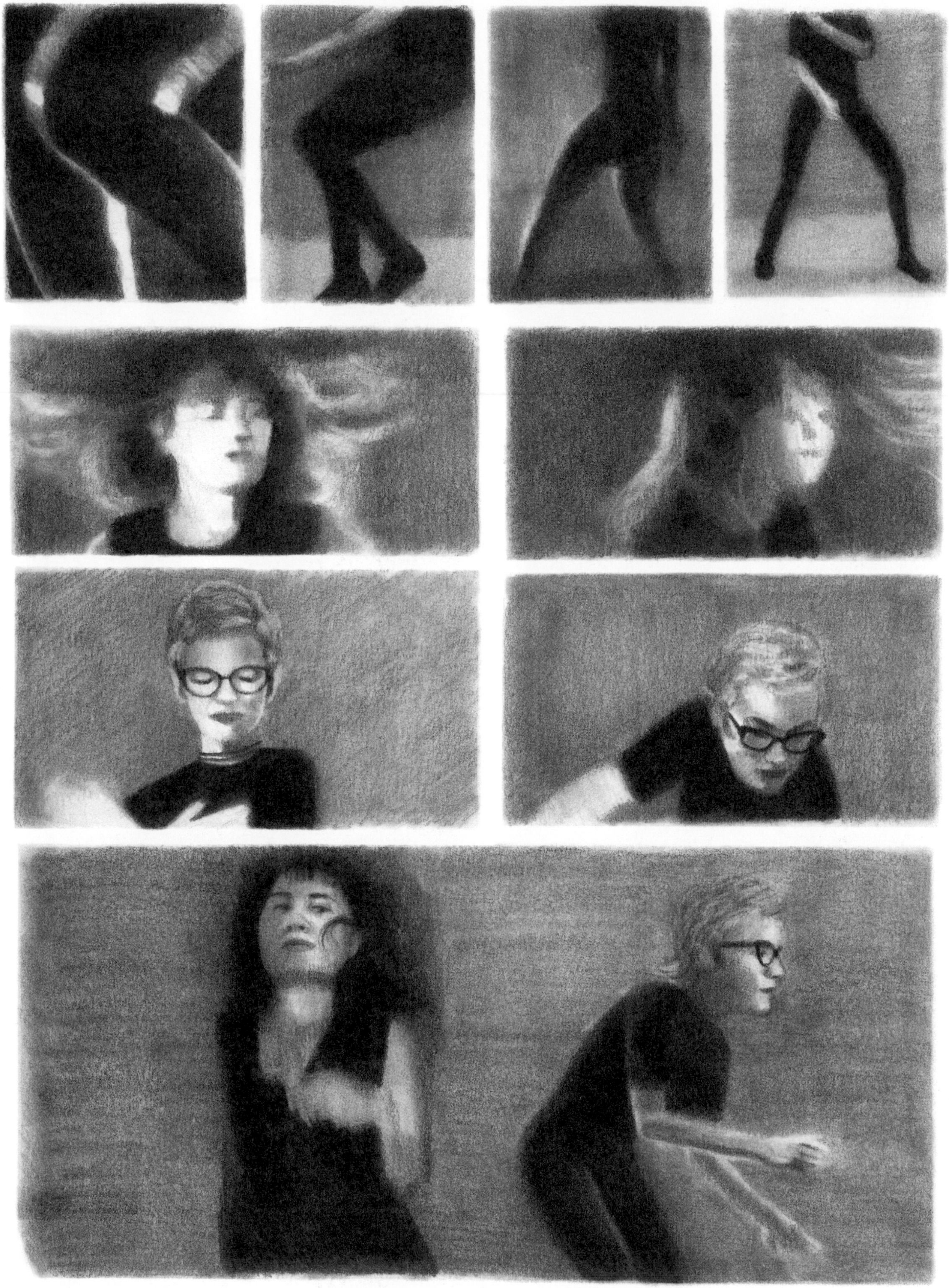

Work out.

Feel good.

Let off steam.

Without pressure and without dieting.

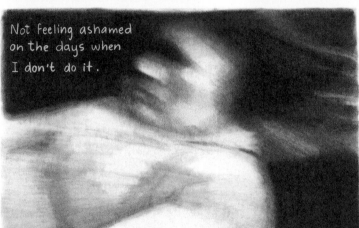

Not feeling ashamed on the days when I don't do it.

Listen to my body.

And be proud of myself.

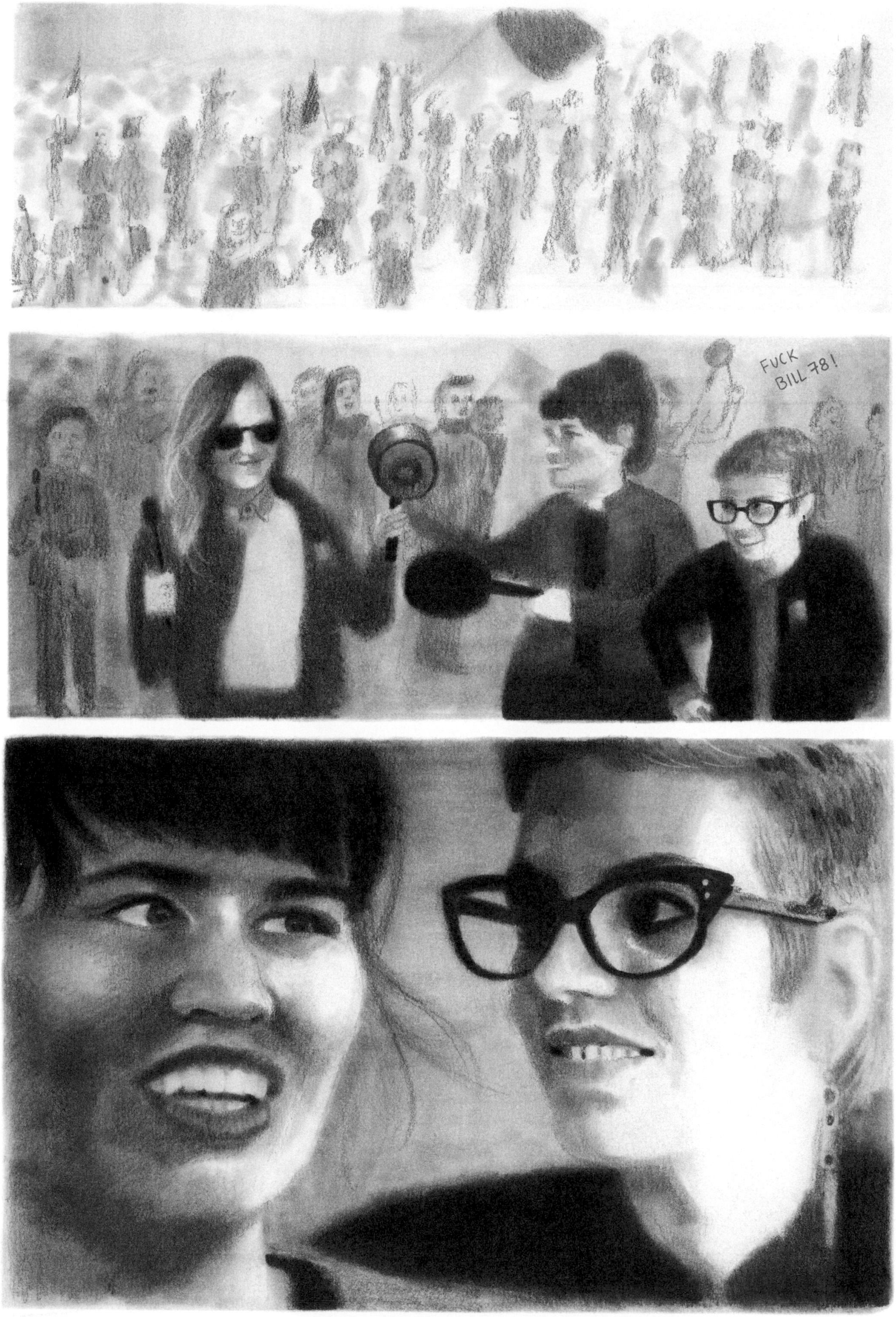
FUCK BILL 78!

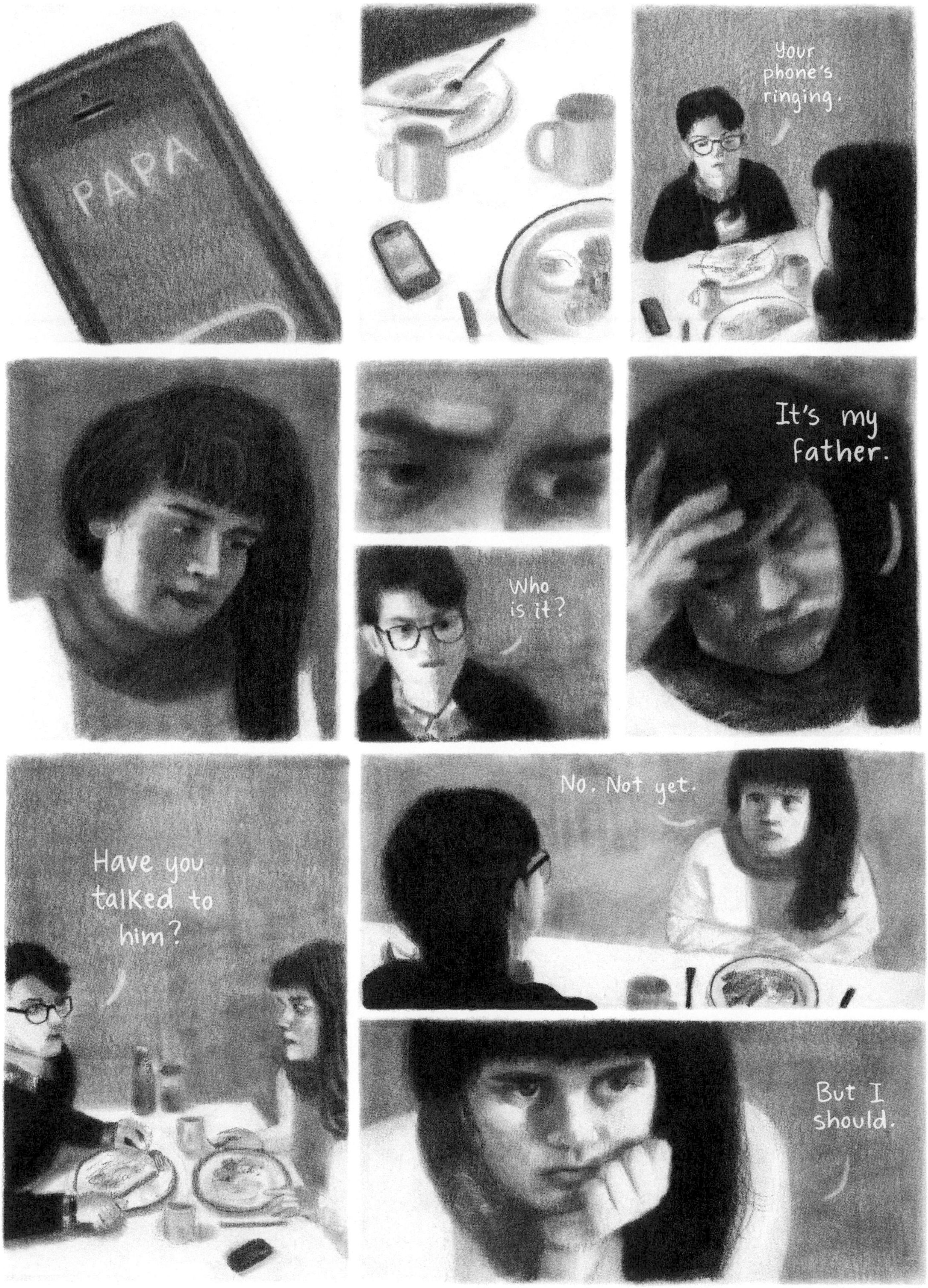
PAPA
Your phone's ringing.
Who is it?
It's my father.
Have you talked to him?
No. Not yet.
But I should.

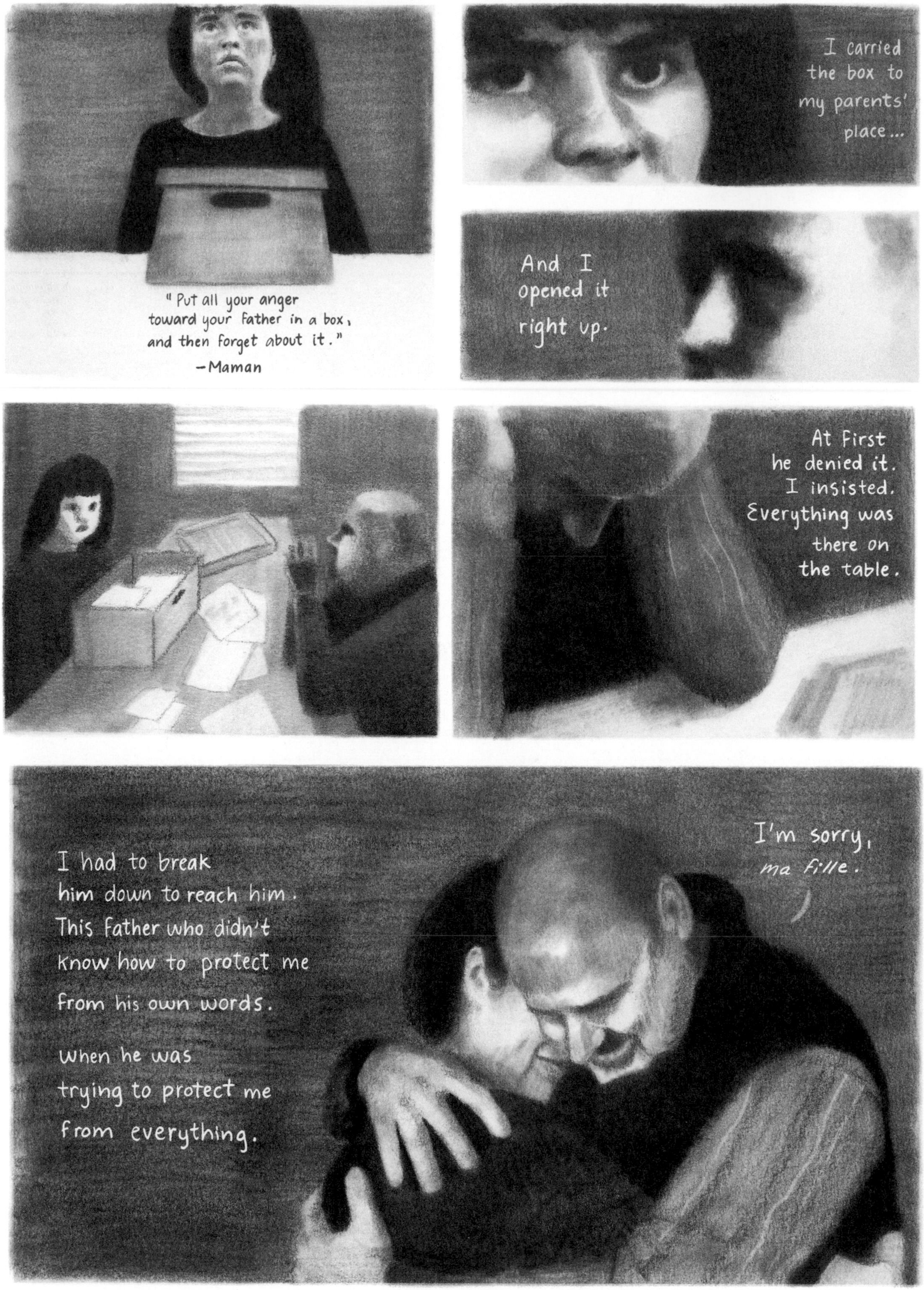
"Put all your anger toward your father in a box, and then forget about it." –Maman
I carried the box to my parents' place...
And I opened it right up.
At first he denied it. I insisted. Everything was there on the table.
I had to break him down to reach him. This father who didn't know how to protect me from his own words.
When he was trying to protect me from everything.
I'm sorry, *ma fille*.

I finally got it out. It was actually pretty easy.

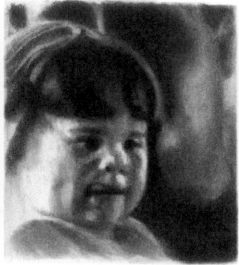

My father thought I should tell this part of our story.

Even if it's ugly.

To show that words can hurt.

Anyway, he and I know the rest of the story.

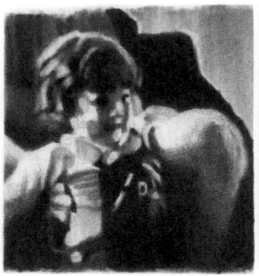

And it's one that's full of love.

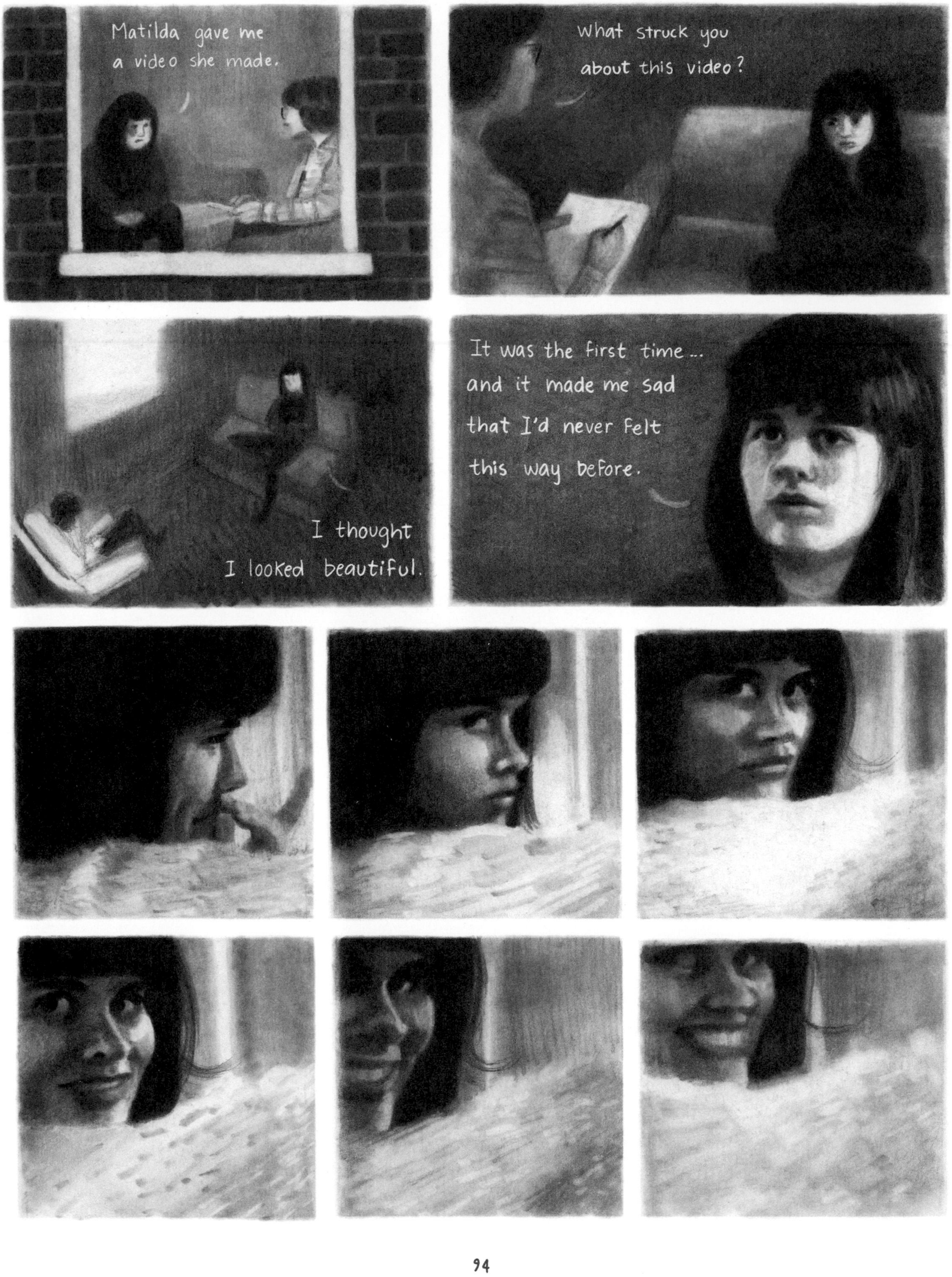
Matilda gave me a video she made.
What struck you about this video?
I thought I looked beautiful.
It was the first time... and it made me sad that I'd never felt this way before.

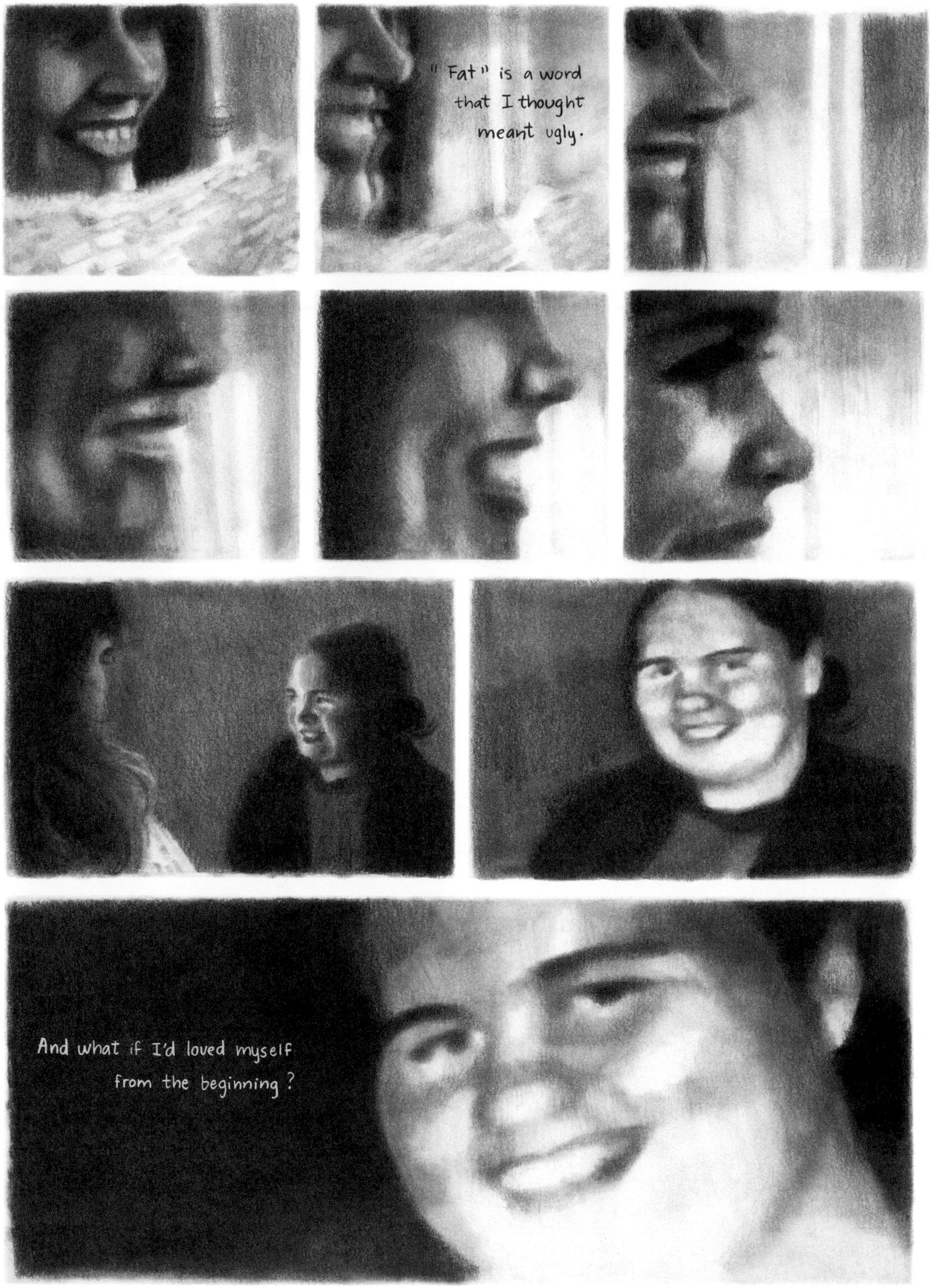
"Fat" is a word that I thought meant ugly.
And what if I'd loved myself from the beginning?

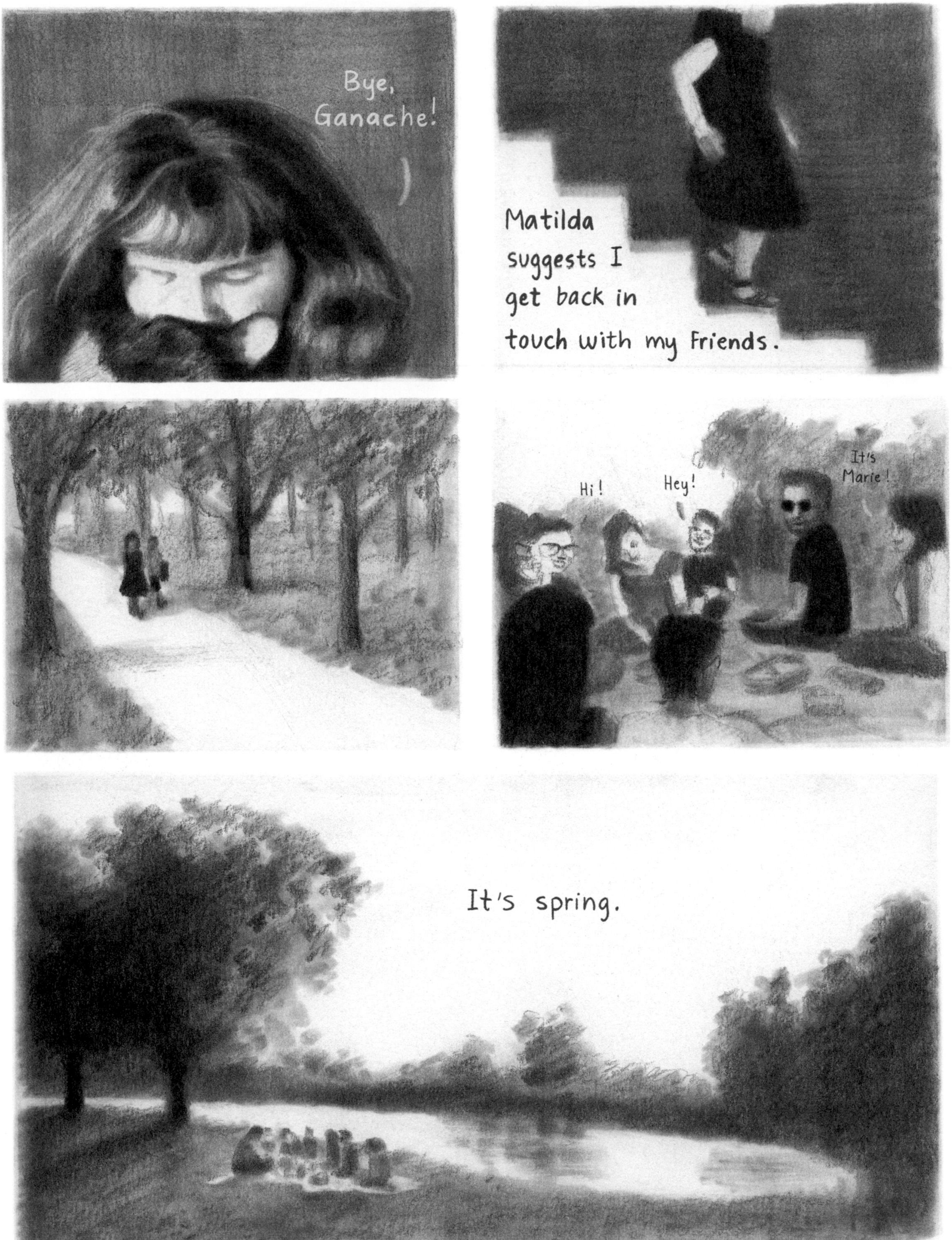
Bye, Ganache!
Matilda suggests I get back in touch with my friends.
Hi!
Hey!
It's Marie!
It's spring.

I would like to give her more.

Be a better friend to her.

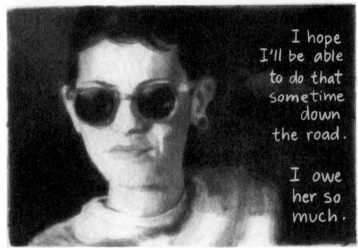

I feel like Matilda carried me when I couldn't move forward anymore.

I hope I'll be able to do that sometime down the road.

I owe her so much.

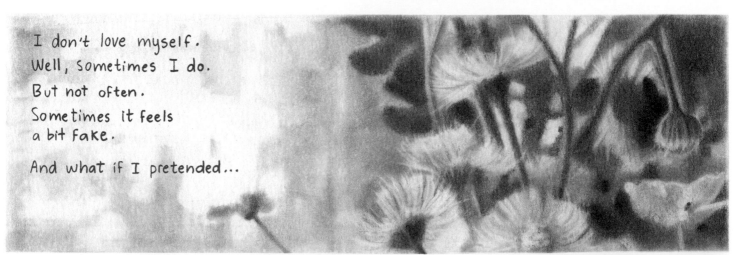

I don't love myself.
Well, sometimes I do.
But not often.
Sometimes it feels
a bit fake.

And what if I pretended...

This is
my body, and
it's beautiful.

Maybe I'll
actually believe
that someday.

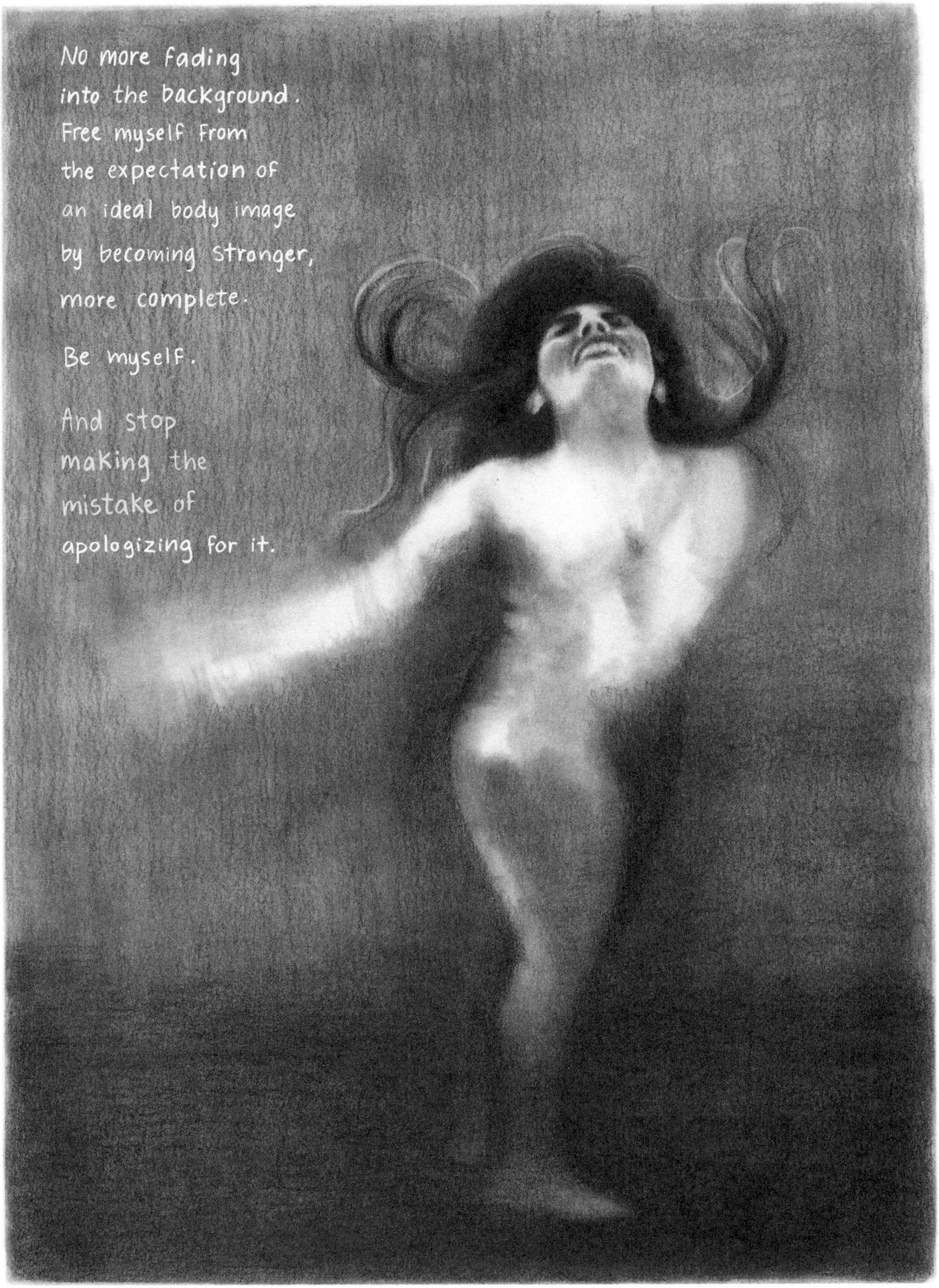
No more fading
into the background.
Free myself from
the expectation of
an ideal body image
by becoming stronger,
more complete.
Be myself.
And stop
making the
mistake of
apologizing for it.

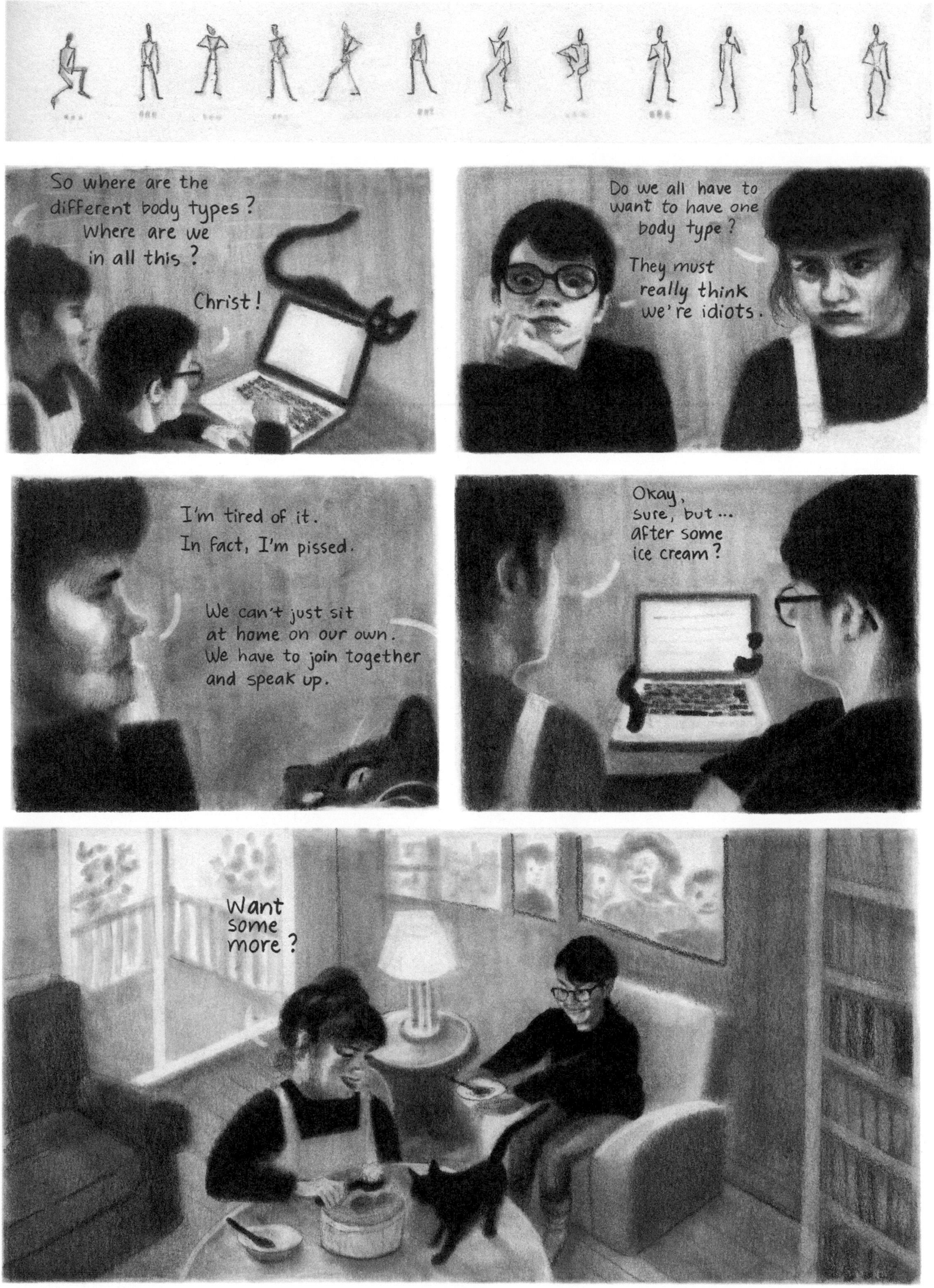

So where are the different body types? Where are we in all this?
Christ!
Do we all have to want to have one body type?
They must really think we're idiots.
I'm tired of it.
In fact, I'm pissed.
We can't just sit at home on our own. We have to join together and speak up.
Okay, sure, but... after some ice cream?
Want some more?

Thank you to Maeva for the help, precious advice, time and friendship.
Thank you, Tristan, for your huge confidence.
Thank you, Maman and Papa, for allowing me to tell this part of our story.
Thank you, Philippe, my love, for your patience.
Thank you, Jimmy, for your expert advice!
Thank you, Gilles, for the beautiful home videos from my childhood.
Thank you, Sarah, for thinking of me and my project!
Thank you to my cat Ganache, whom I love.

When I started my graphic novel, I often thought of the day when I would show it to M. Dubois, my high-school French teacher. And this idea stayed with me during the whole process. Unfortunately, Pierre Dubois died in 2017.

Thank you, M. Dubois, for teaching me to dream, and that in the face of obstacles and missteps, we must carry on.

"I must erect a scaffold, build a ladder,
a ladder tall enough to touch the great blue sky."
— *Swallowed* by Réjean Ducharme,
translated by Madeleine Stratford

Marie-Noëlle

 **MARIE-NOËLLE HÉBERT** lives in Montreal. Largely self-taught, she studied advertising illustration at Collège Salette. She did a series of illustrations for the documentary *Carricks, dans le sillage des Irlandais* by Viveka Melki (Tortuga Films, 2017) and illustrated the children's book *Le voyage de Kalak* (Cuento de luz, 2018). The French edition of *My Body in Pieces*, her first graphic novel, was awarded the Prix des libraires du Québec in 2020.

SHELLEY TANAKA is an award-winning author, translator and editor who has written and translated more than thirty books for children and young adults. She teaches at Vermont College of Fine Arts in the MFA Program in Writing for Children and Young Adults. Shelley lives in Kingston, Ontario.